A
Theory
of
Happiness

A Theory of Happiness

Kim Hyung Seok

BLOOMSBURY PUBLISHING
LONDON · OXFORD · NEW YORK · NEW DELHI · SYDNEY

BLOOMSBURY PUBLISHING
Bloomsbury Publishing Plc
50 Bedford Square, London, WC1B 3DP, UK
Bloomsbury Publishing Ireland Limited,
29 Earlsfort Terrace, Dublin 2, D02 AY28, Ireland

BLOOMSBURY, BLOOMSBURY PUBLISHING and the
Diana logo are trademarks of Bloomsbury Publishing Plc

First published in Great Britain 2026

Copyright © Kim Hyung Seok, 2026
English language translation © Jamie Chang, 2026

Kim Hyung Seok is identified as the author of this work in accordance
with the Copyright, Designs and Patents Act 1988

All rights reserved. No part of this publication may be: i) reproduced or transmitted
in any form, electronic or mechanical, including photocopying, recording or
by means of any information storage or retrieval system without prior permission
in writing from the publishers; or ii) used or reproduced in any way for the training,
development or operation of artificial intelligence (AI) technologies, including
generative AI technologies. The rights holders expressly reserve this publication
from the text and data mining exception as per Article 4(3) of the
Digital Single Market Directive (EU) 2019/790

A catalogue record for this book is available from the British Library

ISBN: HB: 978-1-5266-9769-1; TPB: 978-1-0372-0043-4; EBOOK: 978-1-0372-0047-2

2 4 6 8 10 9 7 5 3 1

Typeset by Six Red Marbles India
Printed and bound in Great Britain by Clays Ltd, Elcograf S.p.A

To find out more about our authors and books visit www.bloomsbury.com
and sign up for our newsletters
For product-safety-related questions contact productsafety@bloomsbury.com

Contents

Foreword   vii

PART ONE: WHERE HAPPINESS DWELLS

Happiness, Here and Now	3
The Price of Enduring Hardship	9
By the Grace of the World	15
Where Does a Happy Life Come From?	23
A Heart That Knows Gratitude	31
A Small Miracle	37

PART TWO: THE POWER TO GROW ON ONE'S OWN

What We Must Give to Those We Love	45
A Lesson We Need	51
Becoming and Doing	55
We Grow Through Our Work	61
Why Honesty, Humility and Positivity Matter in Life	71
What Makes a Life Meaningful?	77
Offering Beauty and Receiving Respect	81

PART THREE: A LOVING AND JOYFUL HEART

    Importance of Loving Wisely   91
    Being a Good Friend   99
    Three Gifts for a Satisfying Life   109
    A Meaningful Life   123
    Recovering the Sense of Leisure   127

PART FOUR: THE ROAD TO THE COMPLETION OF LIFE

    What Fills My Being   135
    A Slightly Melancholy Story   143
    Friendships in the Twilight Years   151
    The Secret to My Health   159
    Health is Built Over Time   165
    Another Name for Death: Life   177
    The Night Train of Life   189
    How Long Should a Person Live?   193

Foreword

I Was Happy Because There Was Love

A pastor from Australia once visited our middle school in Pyongyang while travelling around the world. After delivering a sermon, he said, 'I'll leave you with a riddle. Whoever solves it will receive a prize.' The question he posed was this: 'What is the strongest thing in the world?'

A variety of answers were submitted. Elephants, gravity, the heat and light of the sun. I thought the question was really asking, 'What is the strongest force in life?' So I wrote, 'The strongest thing in the world is justice. If a person lives righteously, they have nothing to fear.'

About a week later, the principal held an award ceremony. 'The strongest thing in the world is love,' was the winning answer. It was submitted by a third-year student older than me. I didn't agree. Justice was stronger than love. Still, the principal called my name and said 'justice' was second place. The prize was a book. I scratched out the word 'Second' in the inscription on the back cover and changed it to 'First'. I was certain that justice was indeed stronger than love.

I lived with that conviction for the next ten years. Soongsil Middle School eventually closed down, and I transferred to a Japanese school. Despite financial hardship, I continued on to university education. I went to study in Tokyo. Many people supported and helped me along the way.

During that time, my thinking began to shift. If those who had helped me were guided only by their sense of justice, I would not have been able to endure the hardships and overcome those crises. It was unconditional love that rescued me. The unconditional love and help I received from professors and pastors, in particular, transformed my thinking. I came to understand that love is stronger than justice, and that justice cannot come to fruition without love.

Several more decades have passed since then, and I've come to experience an even greater epiphany: true happiness that everyone seeks is born of love and nurtured by love. Where there is no love, happiness cannot dwell. The measure of love is the standard of happiness.

Shortly before turning one hundred, I received an award from a university. In my acceptance speech, I said, 'I don't deserve this award. I've never held an important position or accomplished anything particularly great. I know well that there are many more deserving than I. But if I am receiving this award "for the hard work that went into living this long", I will accept it.' I got a big laugh from the audience. Then I confessed, 'But despite all the hard work, I was happy because there was love.' If the hard work wasn't accompanied by love, my life would have been a meaningless, unremarkable one.

In this book, I've recorded stories from the path I walked to this realisation.

I was happy because there was love.
I hope you find happiness, too.

November 2022, Kim Hyeong-seok

PART ONE

Where Happiness Dwells

A person climbing the stairway of life finds meaning in each and every step.

If one fails to find the significance and gratitude of each moment, what joy remains but the thrill of reaching the final step?

Happiness, Here and Now

Everyone seeks happiness. But many mistake happiness as life's ultimate goal. We might think we are working *towards* happiness, but happiness is not something waiting for us in the distant future. If happiness only existed in the future then humans could never be happy, because we live in the present and the future, by definition, has yet to arrive.

Nor can happiness be found in the past. The past has already vanished, and so has the happiness we felt then.

Then where does happiness reside? Happiness only exists in the present, in the here and now. Yet the present is not a fixed point but a passage, a flow. Whether time moves from future to past or past to future, the present is always just a fleeting moment.

If happiness exists at all, it exists only in these passing moments. We are born with a desire and longing for happiness. When we project that desire into the future, we may think happiness lies ahead. But we must not hollow out the present in pursuit of the future, nor should we foolishly let the past rob us of our present.

If happiness can only dwell in the present and the present is a process by which time passes, then happiness, too, must be found in the process. Let's put theory aside and look for examples in real life.

Decades ago, a professor friend from Seoul National University called me. He said he'd just had a phone line installed after two years of being on the waitlist, and wanted to try calling someone. If I wasn't too busy, could we chat for a few minutes? I could hear the excitement in his voice. After this call, his wife was going to try the phone next, and then his eldest daughter.

My friend wasn't the only one excited about opening a phone line. I had the exact same experience when I got my first phone. My family was ecstatic. At the time, there were so many applicants that the phone company had to hold a lottery. The odds of being picked was twenty to one. For several days, our family talked about little else. It really was quite thrilling to wait at the lottery site, hearing people murmur to one another, 'Is it over?' 'Are they done?' 'Wait, one more?' 'Can you see what it says?' And finally, we heard through the speakers, 'Number 489!' We were chosen for a phone line.

As we'd worked so hard to get the phone line, the joy of winning the lottery and getting a phone was enormous. We even discussed where to place it and how best to keep it in good condition.

My friend's family, too, was basking in that small happiness. Young people today might find this story amusing.

But when I look at children growing up in well-off homes today, I'm sometimes surprised. Many of them grow up without ever knowing that kind of joy. Because they've had everything from the start, they take objects in their lives for granted and find no joy in them. If someone gets excited over getting a phone today, they'd likely laugh and think, 'What's the big deal?'

These days, many families own cars. When I bought my first one, I went outside at night to clean it with great care. One friend said he didn't sleep at all the night he bought his car. His wife said, 'Good things really do come to those who wait.'

But my friend's children feel none of that joy. Since cars have always been part of their lives, they see it as nothing special. It's the same with houses. Each step brings happiness as one moves from a rented room to an apartment, then buying a small home in the suburbs, then a bigger one. But young people who are born into wealth and start life in a big house cannot experience the happiness and satisfaction of saving up and moving up that their parents once knew. That's perhaps why many Western families encourage their children to live independently. Only then can they develop the skills to build their lives in their own hands and experience genuine happiness.

If someone were to reach their life's goal all at once, they'd only taste the happiness of the final moment. The true joy of climbing a mountain is in the ascent from the base to the summit. If a helicopter drops you at the peak, you miss the exhilaration of the climb.

A person climbing the stairway of life finds meaning in each and every step. If one fails to find the significance and gratitude of each moment, what joy remains but the thrill of reaching the final step?

Besides, another important point remains. Once a hiker reaches the top of the mountain, they must descend. That descent isn't sad but simply a part of the journey. But life isn't like that. All the joy and happiness are in the ascent. The descent of life always brings sorrow and misfortune.

They say, 'After bitterness comes sweetness.' But turn that around, and we get, 'After sweetness comes bitterness.' Those who have no place further to climb must face decline. That is the tragedy of life.

A poor farmer's son may not begin his life with any advantages, but he has room to rise. But a rich man's son, who began at the top, has nowhere to go but down. This is why youth in poorer countries can be happier than those in wealthier societies. Ascent and growth bring happiness while descent and decline bring with it suffering, discontent and misery. So, we must not treat happiness as a destination, and life as a journey *towards* happiness; it must be discovered and enjoyed within the work and the process of growth.

Those with humble hearts find joy in gratitude and contentment under any circumstances. And those who strive for righteousness experience unique happiness in the strife itself, as it is the process of growth and betterment.

So, does this mean the rich are unhappier than the poor who still have room to grow? Is someone in a powerful position less happy than someone still rising through the ranks? Perhaps so. A person with ten million dollars feels unhappy when they lose three million. But someone with two million who gains three million feels happy. A retiring general may feel he's losing everything, but a colonel promoted to brigadier general is filled with hope.

By that logic, the rising sun symbolises happiness and the setting sun symbolises sorrow. That's nature's law, but human life doesn't always have to follow it. A person can grow in many directions. Once we recognise this, we see things differently. One who has enjoyed material comfort may find new meaning in service or the arts. There is another kind of growth and happiness waiting there. Those in politics or business may find happiness not in power and wealth but in contributing to the community. Many spiritual leaders who lived in poverty found unparalleled happiness.

In short, what we possess matters less than the value we find in life. Acquiring things can be meaningful, but what we give to others and to society often brings deeper happiness. Ultimately, we arrive at the familiar conclusion that happiness is made up of the truthful, meaningful life we live each day, not from desire or illusion. Greed makes happiness elusive, while meaningful volunteer work never brings regret. Therefore, no matter where we are in life, we must strive for meaningful growth. That process will bring true and deep happiness.

It is said that character is the highest form of happiness. One who refines their character and serves others will find joy through this life. Because character is not a vessel that holds happiness, but the very source that creates it.

The Price of Enduring Hardship

Life holds both pain and sorrow on one side, and joy and happiness on the other. But which outweighs the other? Since ancient times, many have believed that joy is fleeting while suffering endures. That a brief moment of satisfaction must be preceded by a long period of hardship.

But if we change our perspective and compare the heights of ecstasy with the depths of suffering, doesn't it seem that the weight of pain is incomparably heavier? When we consider how profound suffering can rob life of all meaning, and how death can devour the very possibility of life, we inevitably fall into despair. Life seems nothing but a path of pain and tribulation. We see this truth played out around us time and time again.

Why must humans bear the burden of suffering? Must we share in sorrow that feels unbearable?

I have watched as my friends endured their own trials.

A friend, himself the only male heir of three generations, lost his only son – a promising young man who, after completing all preparations to study abroad in the United States, took a final trip to Jeju Island and tragically drowned.

A former student of mine lost his life in an accident while on a trip with friends just before he set off to Germany to study. I can still remember his young wife, heavily pregnant, at the funeral. Tragedies are everywhere. And in the face of such immense grief, it's only natural to question whether we must continue to live under such a burden.

What is the meaning of such suffering? Why must humans carry such an unbearable load through life? No one can provide a fundamental solution to this problem. But isn't that precisely why art, philosophy and religion were born?

Still, I believe there are a few views on suffering worth considering. Because if suffering is something that each of us must inevitably face, should we not confront it sincerely and soberly?

First, hardship can enrich lives and build character. Much like the climber who conquers a difficult route, one who courageously overcomes trials and hardships gains a life of meaning and nurtures a character that is nobler for it.

Raising children, for example, brings countless trials. Only those who have walked the path of parenthood truly know the heavy burden and heartache that accompany a parent's journey from their child's infancy to adulthood. Hence the old saying, 'Easy is a life without children.'

But parents who shoulder this weight and persevere through adversity can gain a reverence towards life. They can possess a noble dignity and a character worthy of deep respect.

Second, suffering deepens our love for others. The very fact that loved ones share in our pain is proof of that.

I still remember something a friend who lost his wife once said. After losing his wife and completing all the necessary arrangements, he looked around and thought that everyone in the world suddenly looked like angels to him. While he was buried in loneliness and grief, countless friends came to offer him comfort and sympathy. Having received such love, he said that he'd live a life without enemies from that point on. Indeed, when love is given and received, hatred and jealousy vanish.

To share in another's suffering is thus an act of profound meaning. If such sharing can wash away the sins of the heart and lead to a life filled with reverence and love, then we come to realise just how noble it is to bear one another's burdens and to partake in the pain of those we cherish.

Third, suffering can become a source of hope that promises us a truer and more meaningful life.

The greatest of all suffering is death. There is no agony greater than experiencing the death of someone you love. And yet, even in such irreversible grief, might there not be meaning?

The story of a close relative comes to mind. Tragedy struck in his happy, loving family when his seven-year-old daughter fell gravely ill. The parents poured all their energy and love into trying to save her, but she could not recover.

As the end drew near, the little girl left a clear final message: 'Daddy, I'll go to heaven first and wait for you there. But after I'm gone, you have to stop drinking and start going to church…'

Even on the brink of death, she wished for her father to stop drinking and find meaning elsewhere.

Hearing this, the father replied, 'I promise.' The daughter smiled, content, and closed her eyes.

Afterwards, the father did indeed stop drinking. And he began attending church with his wife.

Today, he is a changed man and the head of a family that others admire. His wife often tells close friends, 'My husband began living a completely new life after our daughter passed away.'

If such unbearable suffering can bring about this kind of transformation, then doesn't that make hardship an even more important facet of life?

My body, my health and even life itself exists thanks to the help and grace of others. And all I need to do is fulfil the one task entrusted to me.

I could not be more grateful for this. How could I ever repay all these people in this lifetime?

By the Grace of the World

In the summer of 1960, the year when the April 19 Student Revolution took place, I visited Chuncheon, a city in South Korea, with Professor Choi Moonhwan, then-president of Seoul National University, and Professor Cho Seung-soon, who taught political science at Korea University. We had been invited as speakers for a lecture event.

After the lecture, we were walking towards the exit of the auditorium when a middle-aged man, who looked slightly older than me, approached and examined my face closely before asking, 'Didn't you give lectures for several days at Deokji-ri in Yeongyu-gun, Pyeongnam Province, many years ago when you were a student at Soongsil School?'

I replied, 'Yes, I did. I'm surprised you remember me from so long ago.'

'I knew it! While listening to your talk today, I had a strong feeling I'd heard you speak before. A previous gathering came to my mind. I couldn't confirm it, of course, but I remembered thinking back then that your teeth were quite unusual. Some of us even joked about it at the time. So when I followed you out of the lecture hall today and saw those same teeth, I just had to ask. I'm really glad I did. Your talk today was very moving as well. Thank you.'

He vanished into the crowd, visibly pleased.

I took comfort in the fact that I was memorable thanks to my crooked teeth.

A few years passed. Two of my upper front teeth had decayed and needed treatment. As two missing front teeth would be a disturbing sight, I thought it'd be best to wait until summer vacation to deal with them. I went to the Red Cross Dental Clinic, where one of my friends worked as a dentist.

After several treatments, he said to me, 'I've done what I could, but I'm not confident about the prosthetics. This is a really unusual case. There's a clinic called Daewon Dental behind Hwashin Department Store. It's run by one of my seniors from school. He's very experienced in difficult prosthetics cases. I'm sorry, but I think that might be your best option.'

Depending on how I looked at it, he either had my best interest at heart or was washing his hands of me. After all, I had never seen anyone with teeth more of a mess than mine.

The dentist at Daewon Dental was very kind. After examining my teeth several times, he said he'd try a special method to preserve the remaining ones.

The process took many visits and a lot of effort, but in the end, the dentist kindly explained everything to me.

'You should be able to use these for at least thirty years. Unless you get into an accident or put too much strain on them... And if they ever rot again, we'll have you fixed up again. So don't worry.'

I checked out my teeth in the mirror. They looked visibly better than before. Even my family, who had been concerned for me, said I looked more handsome than before.

Time eventually fades memories of how things used to look. I lived with those teeth for forty years. Though they were dentures and their colour had darkened over time, I was grateful to have had them for so long.

Eventually, the teeth became unusable. I had no choice but to receive treatment at the dental school at the university where I was working.

My long-time dentist Professor Lee checked out my teeth and said, 'We'll have to remove them and make new ones. This time, we'll match the colour to the adjacent teeth. It'll look better, but it'll make you look quite different. But wouldn't it be better to be a little prettier, even if you don't look exactly like yourself?'

A young dentist beside him laughed and added, 'You're still young at heart, so you should be prettier!'

I couldn't tell whether they really meant to make me look nicer or if they were selling me an option that was easier for them. But then again, choosing to look better rather than worse seems like the obvious choice, even for an old man like me.

Professor Lee showed the younger dentists my old dentures and explained, 'Back then, we didn't have today's materials or techniques. We used to insert metal supports into the teeth to preserve them like this.' I had the feeling they might save it as a historical artifact.

In any case, the treatment that began in late spring continued into the summer. Because it wasn't a molar hidden in the back but a prominent upper front tooth, I had to wear temporary dentures for over two months. It was awkward when speaking or giving lectures, and at home, I sometimes removed them out of discomfort even though I looked grotesque. Well into summer, the gums had firmed up, the prosthetic teeth aligned with the adjacent teeth, and the 'construction' was finished.

Calling dental work 'construction' may sound like an exaggeration, but anyone who's been through major dental reconstruction would agree that the word fits better than 'treatment'. It involves hammering and soldering. The clasps on the temporary dentures have to be reinforced, too.

After the work was done, Professor Lee asked a nurse for a mirror and turned to me as I sat reclined in the chair.

'How does it look compared to before?' he asked.

I wasn't particularly interested in the appearance. I just wanted to know how long they'd last without trouble. But prosthodontists seemed to be invested in improving appearance as well.

So I asked, 'If I'm careful, can these last another ten years?'

'Of course! The colour won't change like the old ones, and the inner part that touches your tongue isn't metal, so it'll feel smoother and more comfortable. It might feel odd at first because it's not living tissue, but over time it'll be hard to tell the difference. There's a limit to how natural they look because your canine teeth are naturally misaligned. But they look much better now! Just compare them with an old photo where you're smiling!'

Even I had to admit my teeth looked better than before. I wouldn't call myself handsome, but it was an improvement.

As I thanked Professor Lee and his team, he added, 'Your wife would've liked your new teeth.'

I turned away and replied with a bittersweet smile, 'She would have. There's no one left to notice or say I look nice. Still, thank you for helping me finally put this lifelong concern to rest.'

He must have thought, *She spent her life seeing your misshapen teeth – she would've been happy to see them finally fixed.*

At home, I brushed my teeth and looked at them in the mirror. They were definitely nicer, but somehow didn't feel like mine. I supposed I'd eventually forget what my teeth used to look like.

Looking back, I realise how grateful I am for all that life has given me. Though it cost some money, countless people took meticulous care of my teeth over the years, allowing me to use them into old age.

And it's not just my teeth. When my greying, thinning hair grows out unsightly, the barber carefully trims it for just a small fee. If barbers all closed their shops saying the pay wasn't worth it, who would take care of my hair?

I also wear glasses, so I rely on eye doctors and opticians. For a modest price, I get expert service and lenses prescribed just for my eyes. Sometimes the lenses come from Germany, and the frames are ordered from Italy. Perfect strangers have helped me with their labour and skill. If opticians ever gave up their work, how could we go on?

That's not all. The clothes I wear and the shoes I walk in are made possible by sheep raised and cattle farmed across the globe. Textiles, tailoring and shoemaking all require the hard work and craftsmanship of experts from many nations. The objects I use daily were made by their labour. What generous, kindhearted people they are.

And it's not just material things. My knowledge and way of thinking were shaped by teachers and friends who loved me, and by the achievements of scholars and artists of the past. They were passed on through efforts hundreds, even thousands, of times greater than my own.

I owe my body, my health and my very life to the help and care of others. All I've ever needed to do is focus on the one task given to me, and people are kind enough to praise me for doing it well. How can I not be thankful?

We humans live by repaying ninety-nine kindnesses with one small offering of our own. I am indebted to so many who've helped me. How could I possibly return the favour to all those who have given so much?

Where Does a Happy Life Come From?

When my friends and I first began our careers as professors, everyone lived in poverty. There was a time when even the secret savings we squirrelled away, so small they would have been chump change for a corporate tycoon or a politician, fuelled both comedy and drama with our wives.

I recall an incident from when I was the editor of the university newspaper. The student reporters were tasked with delivering the manuscript fees to contributing professors as soon as the school issued the paper. Once, a student went to deliver the contributor's fee to Professor K from the College of Theology, but found his office locked. The student asked Professor E next door what to do. E replied, 'He lives in the faculty housing just over the hill. You can pass it on to him there.'

When the student reached Professor K's home, his wife answered the door. The student politely explained that he was delivering the manuscript fee and asked if she could sign or stamp the receipt.

Surprised, she asked, 'The university paper pays?' The student replied that it wasn't much, but the contributors were always compensated. She looked puzzled, stamped the receipt, and asked again, 'Has he received payment from the newspaper before?'

The student had no choice but to answer, 'Yes, there were times the professor came to pick it up himself.'

Later that evening, when Professor K returned home, his wife said with an ominous look, 'I have a bone to pick with you. Please sit down.'

Not knowing what was coming, he asked lightly, 'What's the matter? Are the kids home from school?'

'Does the university newspaper pay or not?'

K was relieved to find that no great disaster had struck. Then he chose to play dumb.

'We're writing for a publication at our own school – why would the professors get paid? Maybe if it was someone outside the school, but the school faculty don't get paid for the articles.'

His wife further cornered him. 'You're claiming you've never been paid, right? And you never will be?'

Too late to change his story now, Professor K answered quickly, 'You're making a big deal out of nothing. I haven't been paid before and won't be in the future, so there.'

He got up to change out of his clothes, but his wife stopped him.

'Sit down a moment. I have something to show you.' She held up the stamped receipt.

Caught red-handed, Professor K had no choice but to mutter, 'How strange… No one told me I'd be paid…' before quickly fleeing the scene. His wife, still fuming, exclaimed, 'How can you lie to me?'

The next day, Professor K called me at school. He confessed to getting an earful from his wife and asked me to make sure the students delivered fees directly to the professors from now on, in case others ended up in similar trouble.

Professor K has since retired and served for many years as the president of a university. He no longer argues with his wife over manuscript fees. But he will also never again experience the joys of that period in life when the couple squabbled over hiding meagre sums of compensation. Maybe someday, he'll tell his grandchildren about those days. If they ask, 'So who won? Grandpa or Grandma?' perhaps he'll reply, 'The one who's guilty always loses,' and the family will laugh about it together.

Professor Cho of Korea University, a well-known economist, once shared his woes in front of younger colleagues. 'These days, there's nowhere left to hide my emergency cash. I kept some in my pants pocket and my watch case, but they were discovered. I even tucked bills into a dictionary, but she sniffed them out somehow. There's just nowhere safe.'

Professor Jung, one of his juniors, offered advice.

'Shall I let you in on a secret? Fold the bills and tuck them inside the sweatband of your hat. No one looks there.'

Everyone wore hats back then. Professor Cho laughed and said, 'That's a great idea. I'll try it. My wife's caught me a few times, and now she's practically a detective, obsessed with finding my hiding spots.'

A few days later, several professors went out to tea together. When the time came to pay, Professor Jung suspected that Cho had hidden cash in his hat. While Cho was in the restroom, Jung peeked into the sweatband and found several bills. He took two and paid for the tea.

The others protested, 'How can we let you pay alone?' But Cho smiled and said, 'No, no, let the young professor treat us today!'

About a month later, Cho grumbled to Jung again.

'Caught again! She even searched inside my hat this time. What's strange is, she only took the bills on one side and left the others. I moved the money into my socks. It's come to this!'

Jung had a hard time stifling his laughter. He couldn't admit what he'd done, nor continue the charade much longer. He'd intended to sneak the tea money back into Cho's hat someday, but that was no longer an option. Jung would have confessed and treated Cho to a nice dinner. He wasn't the kind of person to make a big show of treating friends with someone else's money and try to get away with it.

Eventually, Professor Cho's department adopted a different method: the department secretary began keeping and managing such 'secret funds'. Since the wives often collaborated with one another in these matters, it had become necessary to devise more secure strategies.

I recently ran into Professor S, who was college friends with Cho.

'You don't go out much these days, do you? Understandable, given your age.'

He smiled and replied, 'I should have heeded the saying, "Prepare, and you will not worry." I should've made a secret account before retirement. I handed over all finances to my wife because she's the only one I could trust. But now, my allowance has shrunk to the point where I can't even take a cab home on weekends. And I would never go to my son or daughter-in-law for an allowance. I should've saved something while I had income. Cho, being an economist, prepared wisely and doesn't have to beg his wife.'

He spoke with envy, his smile carrying the same youthful spark as in his adolescence.

Today's salaried workers may not relate to this story. Wealthy CEOs would scoff and say I'm being delusional. But the happiness that came from our modest lives back then – we'll never have that back.

In those days, payday at Seoul National University's College of Liberal Arts meant rows of envelopes printed with salary breakdowns would appear at the accounting office. Many took empty envelopes home to save face after borrowing against their salary in advance.

But the main goal was often to siphon off secret funds. People would deduct small amounts from various categories and fill in altered figures so no one would notice. Close friends living next door would even coordinate their fake figures so as not to get caught.

Professor K at our university had spent many years in Europe and returned with his foreign wife to take a post at our school. On the 25th of each month, even professors who did not have lectures that day came in for payday. Faculty meetings scheduled on that day had perfect attendance.

Professor K, new to the system, once said, 'In Germany, salaries were deposited directly into bank accounts. My wife got to it first, and I had to beg for an allowance. But here, my wife suddenly becomes sweet to me on payday. I usually have to watch myself and try to stay in my wife's good graces, but on the 25th of every month, I get to hold my head high and make demands. For three or four days, she has to be nice to me.'

He concluded that the Korean way was best.

Eventually, someone taught him how to set aside secret funds. He began keeping a stash with the department secretary and withdrew it as needed. Thanks to that secret fund, I was treated to coffee a few times myself.

A few years later, however, our university began depositing salaries into bank accounts as well. Professor K smiled ruefully and said, 'Now that we've gone the German route, I've lost my monthly chance to throw my weight around.'

He's now retired and happily devoting himself to translation work, something he always dreamed of. He probably no longer needs emergency cash. With improved living standards and a wife who knows all the tricks of Korean life, the old ways no longer work. I wonder whether he ever told her about the stash, or if he's taking his secret to the grave.

These days, professors have social standing, secure salaries and financial stability until retirement at sixty-five. Their wives likely have fewer complaints.

TV and newspapers today are filled with ways of making money. 'New intellectuals' invent ways to generate profit. Still, I'm not sure they're any happier than those of us who had once hidden our petty cash from our wives.

Sometimes, I long for those poor but happy days. We were poor, but we weren't slaves to money. There was material lack, yes, but a spiritual richness that made life full. We weren't profit-driven, but we hadn't lost our ideals, and so we didn't suffer from spiritual poverty and lose our way.

Looking back, the happiest life may be one that creates spiritual wealth in the midst of material scarcity. A life where, even with little, one can share much. Perhaps it was that spirit that bore the fruits of today's abundance.

A Heart That Knows Gratitude

Here's a story about a professor I knew well.

When he first went to Japan, he needed to take a taxi. The driver looked very old, so he asked his age. The driver said he was seventy-two years old. Curious, the professor asked if he was still able to drive well at that age. The driver replied that he had passed his physical exam this year as well, and because of his long driving experience, his field of vision was wide enough to drive safely. He added that his lifelong wish was to keep driving until seventy-five, then retire in his hometown to rest.

When the taxi arrived in front of the hotel, the driver got out first, opened the trunk, helped with the luggage, and said, 'Have a pleasant trip,' before driving off in the drizzle. The professor felt a profound gratitude towards this old man. His was a simple job, but he devoted himself wholeheartedly and seemed to have a genuine appreciation for his profession. The man's expression truly reflected his gratitude for having come all the way from a rural village after finishing elementary school and being able to drive in Tokyo until his seventies.

Now, imagine if we were living just after the Korean War. The job market would be far worse than today's unemployment crisis. Most of us would be unemployed because there simply weren't many jobs. Many young people might have been shoeshines, and older people, porters carrying heavy loads. One can still see similar situations in developing countries today. Getting up in the morning and knowing where they're going to work today is all they want.

Given this, shouldn't we be thankful for the work we have? Being grateful for our work does not mean being grateful to the company or government leaders that created the job. It is simply natural to feel gratitude that we have the ability to work and to earn our living.

In the summer of 1947, I crossed the 38th parallel* and moved south. With no place to stay, I lodged in the gateside room of someone I knew. There was no bedding, no coal to warm the room, so I gathered pine needles and pinecones from the mountain to make a fire. At bedtime, instead of taking off my clothes, I had to layer up to keep warm.

---

* The military demarcation line established at the end of World War II, dividing previously Japanese-occupied Korea into Soviet and American occupation zones.

At that time, I was appointed as a teacher at a middle and high school. When my wife heard the news that I had gotten a job, she was so happy that she asked, with tears in her eyes, if we wouldn't have to go to the countryside to buy rice that winter. We'd had to peddle rice from the country to make ends meet.

What is regrettable today is that with worsening working conditions and increasing labour disputes, mutual appreciation and gratitude between labour and management have weakened. This is a deeply unfortunate situation. Throughout my career as a teacher, I observed that friends who worked with a thankful heart, even doing the same tasks, were happier and more productive. In contrast, those who frequently complained and grumbled often brought unhappiness upon themselves and lagged behind in their achievements. Over time, it was common to see that those who were grateful for what they had eventually succeeded as workers and entrepreneurs.

Instead of focusing on dissatisfaction, why not first consider how to improve your skills and experience for a more satisfying job? A worker who only focuses on the negative will remain unhappy their whole life and struggle to find their true place in the workplace and society.

Of course, society is not without contradictions. But those who love their work can overcome these difficulties, and those who are grateful for the jobs and the opportunities they bring are the ones with the ability to transform a society full of contradictions.

As the season of harvest arrives, let it also be a season to find something to be grateful for in everything around us. That will make autumn a season of blessings.

When I tired of seeing with my eyes,
I listened with my ears.
I would empty my mind and listen,
and hear buzzing in both ears.
The sound of power lines humming in the cold winter,
harmonies and melodies filling the universe.

I could hear it whenever I wanted to.
It was my solitary pastime,
one that I could enjoy anytime and anywhere.

A Small Miracle

One day, decades ago, I dropped in at my friend's new internal medicine clinic. It had been at least three months since I'd seen my old friend, who I'd been especially close with, and not only because we'd known each other since middle school.

'Hey, long time no see. How have you been?' he greeted as he led a patient out of an exam room. 'How have you been? I often hear about you through friends, but you didn't come here for a consultation, did you?' he added, worried I had come bearing an ailment after such a long time.

Some time later, he and I sat down for coffee. My friend put on and then took off his reading glasses, saying, 'So old already. I can't read the paper anymore without reading glasses. Do you know other friends of ours who need reading glasses?' He lightly shrugged his shoulders, an old habit of his.

I answered, 'The ones who are older than me, yes. I don't need reading glasses yet.'

My friend laughed and said, 'Usually by about forty-five, one starts using reading glasses. Now, just wait and see. One day, you'll suddenly realise you can't read fine print anymore. It means as you grow old, you should live not by sight but by thought. And when you start forgetting things, it's time to give up your place in life for the next generation.'

I gazed at my friend sitting across from me. Once a middle-school kid who was always picking his nose, he was now a father of seven with greying hair and reading glasses. It felt surreal. But it felt as though we were still the same people we were in middle school.

'By the way, aren't you going to ask me to take your blood pressure? You always have your blood pressure taken when you visit.'

'Well, I'm worried that my blood pressure is always low. Now that I think about it, I must have gotten it from my father. He had low blood pressure his whole life.'

'That might be hereditary. High blood pressure is often inherited. But low blood pressure won't kill you. How about measuring it now since you're here?'

My friend put on his stethoscope and asked me to stretch out my arm. After taking my blood pressure, he said, 'You really are a medical marvel. Your blood pressure can't be this low. I wonder how you're doing all the things you're doing with blood pressure so low. And you don't need reading glasses yet, either. Maybe have a light drink to raise your blood pressure a bit. Not that it'll make a huge difference.' He laughed.

I wondered if that was his way of teasing me because I didn't drink. A patient arrived. I raised my hand and said I'd come again, and left.

On the way home, I remembered the time I had an eye ailment as a child, before I started school. My father warned me not to go out into the bright sunlight, but I didn't listen. So he locked me in the dark attic we used for storage. He ordered me to stay there until the sun went down.

That was the longest, most boring day I had ever experienced before or since. When my mother came in and laid out a sleeping mat, I just lay down. But lying down had its own secret pleasure unknown to others. Closing my eyes quietly for a minute or two, the darkness before me would open up wide and high like the autumn sky.

Looking back, the images that emerged when I closed my eyes back then was my universe. From one side of that space to the other, countless shapes of light flowed in procession. The moving shapes looked exactly like shooting stars, and sometimes I would try to control their speed to drift slowly. Countless yellow dots flowed at steady intervals against the dark expanse.

After watching for a long time, if I wanted to see something else, I would gently rub my eyes, and everything would disappear at once. A minute or two would pass, and new images would appear. Rows of flame-shaped lights close to ovals marched sideways. Sometimes their shape and colour would slightly change, covering my entire vision like a flock of silent birds in flight. I repeated this for twenty or thirty minutes at a time. Then, when I opened my eyes, everything vanished. The mysterious space that had shown me my universe returned to the darkness of the lightless room.

Time was still endlessly available. This pastime could continue indefinitely. It was a fun way to turn my father's punishment into a game. When I tired of seeing with my eyes, I listened with my ears. I would empty my mind and listen, and hear buzzing in both ears. The sound of power lines humming in the cold winter, harmonies and melodies filling the universe. I could hear it whenever I wanted to. This was my solitary pastime, one that I could enjoy anytime and anywhere.

I would transform this sound into whatever I wished. Sometimes it sounded like a plaintive melody, other times the voice of a friend calling me, a ghost weeping or a young lady singing. Sometimes it simply sounded like a melody and harmony filling the universe. After a while, the sound would suddenly cut off. But if I wished, I could always hear it again.

This was not just a one-time occurrence on the day I was confined to the attic. It was my own game, a solitary pastime I could enjoy anytime and anywhere. On summer afternoons without friends, after waking from a nap, it was a lonely shadow of fantasy that I would enjoy for long stretches.

I shared this story with a few people, but hardly anyone had had the same experience. Some even gave me a strange look that said, 'Were you a little nuts as a child?' Afterwards, I came to the conclusion that the things I saw and heard were probably due to a frail constitution I had from birth. I rarely checked my blood pressure in the past, but I suspect it was even lower then than it is now.

Back home later that day, I briefly mentioned my health to my mother, who was chatting with her grandchildren. She said in her usual way, 'Have you ever lived a single day in good health?' Then she turned to my children and said, 'I never dreamed your father would live to be twenty. Doctors gave up on him, saying he wouldn't grow up to function like a normal person. But seeing you raise your children now, maybe nothing is impossible in this world. I agonised day and night, wondering what sin I had committed to bear and raise such a child…'

The children didn't seem surprised. It was a story they often heard from Grandma. My mother's words are true. Whether in my twenties, thirties, or now, I feel little difference in my health. I have always stuck to my healthy routines and taken good care of myself, which is how I can do what I want nearly as well as others and rarely get sick.

Everyone who knows my past thinks of my present health and life as a kind of small miracle. But I prefer to believe that devotion to simple habits can always create small miracles.

PART TWO

The Power to Grow on One's Own

A good family is not defined by wealth or appearances.
When a home can nurture a sense of social responsibility,
a concern for neighbours and society,
the suffering of both individuals and society can be greatly reduced.

What We Must Give to Those We Love

Several years ago, about twelve university students from the southern United States visited our home in the winter. Their professor had asked if he might introduce them to a Korean home and meal, so we hosted them for an evening.

One of the students was dressed in extremely shabby clothes. Even his shoes were noticeably worn.

My wife asked the professor, 'Does that student come from a poor family?'

To which the professor replied, 'What makes you say that?'

My wife explained that his tattered clothing and shoes gave that impression.

The professor then said, 'No, in fact, that student is probably one of the wealthiest of the group. His father owns a ranch in Texas and his mother runs another in Mexico. They have more cattle than they can count, and they sell them by the hundreds. But he dresses that way because of his parents' upbringing. Where he comes from, the wealthier the family, the more strict they are with money. Very few families give their children more money than they need or pay tuition in full without conditions.'

We have a rough idea of how Western families operate when it comes to money. Children are often given weekly allowances from a young age. If they need extra money, they borrow it or receive help from their parents under certain conditions. It's rare for parents to cover the full cost of the children's college education unconditionally. Barring special circumstances, college students are expected to earn their own living expenses. Raised this way, they develop financial independence and learn the value of money early on in life. The parents aim to help their children develop an ability to manage money, for only then can they pass down the family business to their children knowing it will be in good hands.

This is something our society has already begun to understand, and an issue we must deeply reflect on. There are countless cases where young people who came into money quickly have become entangled in gambling or drugs and don't take responsibility for themselves. Where does the problem originate? One could think that this is a family matter, but the underlying problem may apply to all of us parents.

Carl Hilty once said that if the only value a family, no matter how wealthy, can teach their children is how to build wealth and enjoy life, such an upbringing cannot produce truly great people. But the poorest of households can produce remarkable individuals if they teach their children to care for their neighbours and be invested in their community. An exemplary home, then, is not one that gives much by way of wealth, but one that instils a sense of social consciousness in its children.

With this in mind, we can understand why so many wealthy young people today, who live selfishly and without much thought for others, grew up without learning that genuine social responsibility. Speaking in terms of numbers, a person with a 90-point character can manage up to 89 points of wealth. A person with a 60-point character can handle up to 59 points of wealth. But someone with a 40-point character who inherits 80 points of wealth becomes miserable trying to manage wealth he did not earn and brings harm to society as well.

Yet we still often prioritise passing on material wealth over nurturing our children's character and humanity. Sometimes we even restrict their personal development just to protect that wealth. Isn't that what we now see playing out in the world around us? Those with large fortunes aren't the only ones making these mistakes. Any parent who neglects their children's character while pushing them to pursue wealth, fame, status or success is making the same error – and will face the same result.

What we must first give to those we love is not material possessions, but an environment conducive to the development of their character and the cultivation of their humanity. Material things are important only as a means to this vital end. If we can instil the value of money and a sound sense of social responsibility, then much of the personal and societal misfortune brought on by wealth could be prevented.

If you are willing, nothing is impossible.
If you try, nothing is out of reach.
If necessary, don't stop after seven tries – try ten.

A Lesson We Need

I spent my adolescence in Pyongyang. One day in my third year at Soongsil School, the vice principal stood before us and said, 'As many of you may already know, today will be our principal's last day at this school. He will now come forward to offer his final address.'

Soongsil School was founded by American Presbyterian missionaries. It had produced many nationalists and during the Japanese occupation of Korea it had been persecuted by the Japanese authorities for refusing to perform the mandatory Shinto shrine rituals. As a result, our principal was dismissed from the position, and the school would no longer be run by the missionaries.

That morning, Japanese police surrounded the auditorium, while detectives sat by the phones in the room behind the auditorium, prepared to call in reinforcements if necessary. Into that tense silence stepped our principal, an American missionary who'd adopted the Korean name Yun San-on. He stood before us in the auditorium and shouted, '*Hara!* – Act!' He stood still, raised his fist into the air and shouted again, '*Hara!*' He repeated this five times. Tears began to stream from his eyes. Even so, he shouted the phrase at the top of his lungs two more times – for a total of seven. Then he lowered his hand, bowed and left the stage.

We, still children, were nervous and confused. I even thought to myself, 'Why didn't he say something more interesting?' And so, the principal left our school, and the institution shifted to conform to the Japanese educational policies.

That was ages ago. But we all still remember that moment – his raised fist and the seven cries of '*Hara!*' My classmates and I reminisced about it for years to come.

We didn't understand his message at the time. We were too young. But now that we are older, we can finally grasp what he was trying to tell us. His message wasn't anything profound but a call to action. Why sit quietly, hoping that 'time will change things', or 'waiting to see what happens', or thinking 'things might improve eventually'?

He was trying to tell us to act with resolve. That if we work hard, we can succeed in our studies, regain independence for our country and start a new chapter in history. He was imploring us not to remain passive and to end this injustice with our own hands.

He had arrived in Korea early in life. During the March 1st Movement in 1919, he printed and distributed copies of the Declaration of Independence in the basement of his home. Because he continuously supported Korean independence, he was monitored and persecuted by the Japanese. Had he not been a foreigner, he would have been imprisoned.

Korea may have seemed too passive, too timid, too lacking in initiative in his eyes. So he implored us, children though we were, to live with courage, to take initiative, to believe in our own power to create and to bring about change. And behind his seven cries of '*Hara!*' was a belief that our country would one day be free from occupation.

Now that I am past the age of one hundred, I believe the lesson we need most is still this: 'Act'. If you are willing and able, nothing is impossible. If you try, nothing is out of reach. If necessary, don't stop after seven tries – try ten. The youth of today must become the generation that breaks new ground and embraces their infinite potential.

*We must face reality head on
with the conviction and courage to act.
Without the willingness to act,
one cannot succeed.*

Becoming and Doing

Not long ago, I revised a book I had written several years earlier for a new edition. As I was proofreading, something struck me as odd: I had used the word 'become' far more often than I expected. When I tried replacing 'to become' with 'to be', I found that more than half of the instances could be changed without loss of meaning. Why had I relied so heavily on 'become' when 'be' was available?

This thought occurred to me: matter is typically understood in terms of 'being'. A desk or a book simply *exists* in place. But living things like plants and animals are not defined merely by their being; their defining feature is growth. Growth belongs to a higher dimension than mere existence. Humans, in turn, not only exist and grow, but create both material things and culture.

'Become' sits between the concepts of 'being' and 'growing'. If 'being' is the most basic state of existence and 'growing' the state above that, one could say that 'becoming' is located on the 1.5 level. It's a continual process. 'Doing', meanwhile, is located between 'growing' and 'creating' – the 2.5 level.

Historically, Koreans have favoured 'become', while Westerners have built their language and worldview around 'do' as the auxiliary verb. Can societies shaped by centuries of using 'become' develop in the same way as those shaped by 'do'? This preference may reflect a core value of the pioneering spirit of the West.

Why does the Korean language favour 'become'? The philosophy of I Ching is the philosophy of becoming. The laws and cycles of the natural universe repeat, and this repetition breeds a sense of inevitability and a worldview grounded in fate. Reverence for nature is central to Eastern tradition, and belief in this cyclical order may have made fatalists of us, whether we realise it or not as it's grounded in a kind of acceptance and passivity. Hence, the frequent use of 'become' over the more active 'do'.

After all, can human effort make the sun rise in the west or bring autumn before summer? Eastern thought teaches that to see the world wisely and live well, one must recognise the limits of human artifice and trust in the greatness of nature. Thus, many have come to believe that what humans do is often a kind of falsehood, while nature in its unaltered form is closer to the truth. In this sense, Eastern thought may offer a wiser, more transcendent standpoint.

A THEORY OF HAPPINESS

The teachings of Laozi and Zhuangzi, two pillars of ancient Chinese philosophy who encourage us to flow naturally with the world's transformations, still resonate deeply in us.

The West, meanwhile, has explored both microscopic and vast realms, unlocking the mechanisms of molecules, blood cells and atoms and pioneered the computer age. They explored the world as well, sailing past Africa to the Indian Ocean, crossing the Atlantic to discover the Americas, exploring the poles and eventually landing on the moon. The world has changed, of course, and now Asian countries are reclaiming leadership in many areas but Western ideals placed great faith in the human capacity to shape and remake the world. The result was the pioneering spirit of modern Western society – a belief in doing that drove ambition and built history. It's a viewpoint that privileges action and ambition, counter to Eastern ideals that more easily embrace simplicity and harmony without resisting or forcing the natural rhythms of life.

Every worldview has its pros and cons. It would be foolish to say the Western mindset is inherently superior. But fundamentally, humans are finite creatures that create infinite potential. To forfeit that potential is to invite our own ruin. Human fulfilment lies in using our ability to the fullest and continually creating new things.

We must embrace the confidence and courage to 'do' in our lives. Only those who embrace the spirit of 'doing' will ever reap the full benefits of 'becoming'. The two are mutually dependent.

*If we continue to grow,
we can live valuable and meaningful lives and contribute to society.
A person's life is defined by what and how they do things.
The growth of a human being depends on what we do and how we do it.*

We Grow Through Our Work

Several years ago, a German high-school student stayed at our home for a year as part of a student-exchange programme. During that time, we noticed that the student was extremely frugal. As one of my children said, 'Our friends say we're stingy, but this German student is in a whole other league.'

I once asked her, 'Who bought you your camera?'

'I did,' she replied. 'I didn't eat ice cream for a year and a half so I could save up for it.'

Whenever we travelled as a family, she would insist on finding the cheapest lodgings. 'There must be a cheaper place…' she'd say, dragging us around to look for more economical options.

One day, we took the bus into town, and when the conductor came by, she pulled out twenty won to pay her fare. She assumed I would only pay for myself. I said, 'When you're riding with me, I'll pay your bus fare. Save your money,' and gave the conductor forty won. She was visibly delighted to have saved twenty won from her 2,000-won monthly allowance. From then on, every time I had errands downtown, she would try to save another twenty won by saying, 'Are you going into the city today? Can I come with you?'

We were curious what she was saving up for. We found out later that she bought drawing paper, pencils, erasers and crayons, and took them to a children's hospital every Saturday. She handed out supplies, drew pictures, played and sang songs with the children. When it was time to return to Germany, she had become so attached to the children that she couldn't stop crying as they said goodbye. It was clear she had been raised in a home with strong values and social consciousness.

One day, she came to me with a question. 'Our teacher asked us to raise our hands if we wanted to go to university after high school. All sixty-one students raised their hands. Do all of us really need to go to university?'

I asked, 'Don't German students attend university after high school?'

'In my class of twenty four, only four or five plan to go to university.'

In Germany, university tuition fees are minimal, and meals at campus cafeterias cost about half of what restaurants charge. Still, many choose not to attend university. Those without clear academic or leadership goals enter the workforce right out of high school. They see university as a place for research and seek to further their professional growth in society and the workplace.

In Korea, we tend to believe that all education and personal growth happens in school. That's why people often think that graduation marks the end of learning. One attends high school to get into university, and university degrees are a means to getting a job.

This is a deeply misguided view. The body may stop growing around age twenty, but the mind can continue developing well into our seventies and eighties so long as we keep working at it. To give up on lifelong growth at such a young age is a tragedy.

So, how do we achieve social and professional growth?

First, we must take an interest in the intellectual foundations of our work. A technician must do more than keep machines running, but understand why the machine works the way it does, what steps lead to which results. Don't just drive a car – understand the principles behind it. It's the same for clerical workers. Beyond processing documents and getting approvals, they should know the purpose of each document and the implications of its contents.

Too often, people make things without a second thought, assuming it's enough that the machine is running. But some workers go further and understand how the product is used and what it's for. That understanding becomes the fuel for innovation to make things better and more convenient. Understanding fuels growth.

When such thought, observation and improvement become second nature, people grow without even realising it. They become better technicians, more capable administrators and creative contributors. Rather than just going through the motions of work, they think before they make decisions and reflect on their choices later. This is how one grows through work.

Leaders work more with their minds while entry-level jobs tend to be manual and repetitive. But it's also true that entry-level workers who think and study diligently will rise to higher positions. There is no doubt about that.

Second, the idea that we grow alongside our work means we must not neglect our personal development while pursuing our careers. If a person's potential is 90, they can handle tasks up to level 89. But if their capacity is only 70, they will never exceed level 69 no matter the task. Therefore, the most essential thing for us is to cultivate our capabilities.

We must never give up on continuous learning and growth. If a business owner does not study economics, if a manager makes no effort to understand human relationships or if a trader ignores the trends of the global market, what outcomes can we expect? We must all strive for personal growth with utmost dedication.

A THEORY OF HAPPINESS

I visited Tokyo in the summer of 1972. While strolling through the Ginza district, I suddenly remembered a bookstore called Kondo in the area. But then I thought, 'It must be gone by now. Back then a single tsubo* of land cost 200,000 yen; now it's over 9 million yen. There's no way a bookstore could have survived here.' But to my surprise, the store was still standing. Overjoyed, I stepped inside and was shocked by what I found. The store was packed. People stood two-deep at the shelves, browsing the carefully curated selections. Because of the heat and the lack of space to browse, I had to step outside. At that moment, a thought crossed my mind: 'People in this neighbourhood are reading just as much as they did thirty years ago. No wonder this society continues to grow.'

Indeed, we must devote ourselves to studying and growing, even if it means setting aside slivers of precious time in our busy lives. This will help enrich our lives in addition to improving our professional abilities.

Third, what we seek is balanced personal growth. No one can be perfect in every way, but we must avoid serious flaws in character or extreme imbalances in personality.

Once, I was invited to give a special lecture to newly hired bank employees who had been assigned to work

---

* A unit of area, roughly equivalent to 3.3 square metres.

mainly with digitised data analysis. They had been immersed in computer training for several months and were to continue that work indefinitely. During that time, they all began to feel the same problem of mental fatigue and a yearning for emotional relief.

Humans are not machines. When we are emotionally drained, we often turn to drinking or leisure activities to unwind. But if this becomes habitual, we drift away from a healthy, well-rounded personal life. One common ailment of modern life is the impoverished humanity of a self that must handle repetitive, mindless tasks day after day. This can lead to the loss of one's sense of self.

People who work in urban settings must find meaning and fulfilment in their work. If the purpose of work is to nurture well-rounded character, then we must never forget that we are not only workers but human beings. Emotional maturity creates positive feelings and genuine bonds between people, so we must never neglect personal development and enrichment.

If we are surrounded by emotionally barren or insensitive colleagues, it's not only their loss but a challenge for everyone around them.

What, then, can we do to be more in touch with our emotions and be patient with one another? The arts and literature are among the most effective means. Frivolous pastimes can tire the mind, but artistic hobbies encourage creativity and contribute to a well-rounded personality. Reading enriches and elevates our inner lives and enables both spiritual growth and human fulfilment.

Fourth, an essential element of growth is social development. We often use the term 'social maturity'. Some people may be in their fifties or sixties physically, but in terms of social grace and lived wisdom, they are still immature.

Those who lack social growth have trouble feeling gratitude or compassion in their relationships with others. They do not understand the importance of being decent and fail to value the emotions and perspectives of those around them. They interact with others in a brusque and ungracious manner, always self-centred and entitled. Such people cannot offer kindness or uphold basic etiquette and inevitably fail to form strong bonds with others. Social growth can be the first step in remedying this problem. We must make it a habit to engage in life with others in a harmonious, cooperative spirit, bringing joy to those around us and supporting one another.

As the saying goes, shared joy is doubled, shared sorrow is halved. This captures the essence of human relationships. Those who give generously will receive in abundance. A life devoted to serving and helping others is the very path to social growth, for social growth takes place through relationships.

Those who cherish human connections and care for others strive to make their communities better places in all areas of their lives. In the workplace, they uphold its integrity and work to improve it. In their relationships, they seek to strengthen bonds. They show patience in the process and initiative when it comes to supporting family, colleagues and society.

We must live in a way that values order and supports others in both the workplace and society. If we continue to grow as individuals in this way, then we not only lead meaningful and noble lives but also elevate the value of our professions and contributions to society. A human life is defined by both *what* we do and *how* we do it.

When we remember that each person's growth is directly linked to society's growth, we must carry the responsibility of social development with even greater resolve.

*With diligence and courage,
    one can accomplish their goals and more.
Isn't this bold, affirmative spirit
    the greatest weapon youth can possess?*

Why Honesty, Humility and Positivity Matter in Life

Like a student hoping to attend a good school, or a young couple hoping to build a good home, we all hope for better lives and better workplaces.

What's odd, though, is that while people are dedicated to nurturing their families, many people in the workforce lack the will and conviction to make their workplaces better. Some even seem to have lost their gratitude towards their chosen professions. Others make it their job to be the voice of opposition at work. Those who lack appreciation for their jobs cannot experience the happiness the work offers. People who cannot feel grateful for their professions ultimately fail to unlock the path to success.

My mother married into our poor family and endured great hardship as a peddler. In return, she received the deep respect and love of fifty descendants in her later years. My wife crossed the 38th parallel and survived the Korean War. She never hesitated to go to the countryside to buy rice and vegetables to sell in the city to keep us afloat through the difficult years. As a result, she was loved and cherished by many children during her life.

If we only expect to benefit from the work of others and hope that someone else will make our workplaces better, finding meaning and joy at work becomes a challenge.

One condition for building a better workplace is to make it a more joyful space, and this cannot be accomplished without the efforts of all its members, employees and executives alike. Happiness is a gift given to those who create it.

What makes us happy? Above all, happiness comes from the way we relate to one another. If one looks at the world through a negative lens, one cannot find joy. When we are selfish and wary of others, we cannot hope for fulfilling relationships.

To build good relationships with our work colleagues, there are a few attributes we ought to cultivate. Honesty, integrity and commitment to the work are key. If we are not honest, we lose the trust of our coworkers. If we fail to act with integrity, we lose the respect of friends and supervisors alike. A lack of honesty implies the possibility of deceit. Questionable integrity makes collaboration difficult. In personal relationships and in business, the most important elements are trust and cooperation. If others don't trust me and I cannot work with others, there is little we can accomplish together. Such arrangements bring harm to the workplace.

We can derive happiness from work only when we are honest and positive. Only then can work bring joy to both ourselves and to those around us.

To increase the harmony and joy in our professional lives, we must all become more humble. Some people are naturally humble and conscientious. These virtues often belong to those who were raised in families who nurtured these traits. But many have overinflated egos and feel frustrated when others do not give them the recognition they believe they deserve. At one time, there were tensions in the public service sector caused by those who had passed the civil-service exam. Passing the exam merely meant one had studied and performed well on a test. The test score did not elevate their worth as workers or human beings, and yet those who entered government jobs through the civil-service exam looked down on their superiors and colleagues who were hired through different routes. Such a workplace cannot grow in harmony or happiness. But if those individuals approach their roles with humility and sincere effort, they will earn others' respect, serve as role models and naturally rise to positions of leadership.

Being humble for the sake of appearance is not the goal. True humility is the ability to assess oneself fairly, knowing one can always find ways to grow and consistently working towards it. There's an old saying that the rice plant bows its head as it ripens. This humility is essential for happiness both at work and at home.

Other crucial conditions we must add to help both our workplaces thrive and ourselves flourish are positivity and hard work. People are capable of more than they think when they believe in themselves and face challenges with courage. But if one approaches a task thinking it can't be done or that it really isn't their responsibility, it can bring harm not only to themselves but to the entire team.

We must approach tasks with the belief that we are capable of handling it, and that our society is capable of reaching the goals we set. An athlete enters a competition to win. There can be no other goal. Likewise, we must always approach our responsibilities with a can-do attitude, avoiding pessimism or passivity, and facing work with confidence and drive.

Earlier generations built the foundation of today's Korean economy with the slogan, 'We can make it happen if we try.' In recent years, however, that spirit has eroded to, 'Can we make it happen if we try?' And now, some young people lean further still towards 'Should I even try?'

The positive attitude that we can and must take on what lies ahead is the greatest power of youth.

*One who does the job entrusted to him without seeking recognition,
One who grabs every opportunity that comes his way,
One who gladly gives up one's wealth to help those in need
– which has led the most valuable life?*

What Makes a Life Meaningful?

Let me tell you about three people I've known.

One of them is the manager of a factory located deep in the mountains, far from Seoul. After graduating from an engineering school, he joined a company and dedicated all his energy to building a factory in the years when the country was recovering from the Korean War. In the process, a design error and lack of experience led to an accident. He himself was injured, and the junior engineer he had recruited died shortly afterwards.

The factory was eventually completed, and after three years of operation, he saw good results. As a reward for his efforts, he was offered a promotion to the company's headquarters in Seoul. After preparing to move, he visited his late colleague's grave. But he found that he could not bear to leave. He had sent a younger man ahead of him into the next world.

He found himself making a vow on the grave. 'We were both born into a poor society filled with trials, and yet you died before me because I was the one who brought you here. How can I ever be forgiven for that? May you rest in peace knowing I will work twice as hard and do the work you were meant to do as well…'

He gave up his transfer to Seoul. He decided instead to dedicate himself to honouring his colleague's memory and to the construction and design of factories.

When I met him, he was already quite old. And yet, he was still serving as the manager of a new plant. As if he had been born for this task, he remained in the mountains, quietly building facilities for the future. To this day, whenever I think of him working in silence, far away from his family, I feel a deep sense of reverence. He is a rare example of a person who works for the sake of the work itself.

Another person I know was a university professor, who had long harboured ambitions to enter politics. While serving on the faculty at school, he always preferred administrative positions – first department chair, then dean, and ultimately, he hoped to become president of the university. He never missed an opportunity to pursue positions of authority. While teaching lofty ideals to his students, he spent his vacations abroad, flattering and currying favour with those in power.

Of course, people around him were not blind to this self-serving, ambition-driven behaviour. His colleagues and university administrators began to distance themselves from him, and students derided him as a sycophantic professor. Still, he was skilled at seizing opportunities and eventually succeeded in becoming a member of the National Assembly.

He flattered his superiors with obsequious loyalty while presenting himself to young intellectuals as a champion of democracy. He deftly played both sides. But such a double life could not last forever. In time, both communities rejected him. I don't know what he's doing now.

Yet some people still praise him. Some talk of him as a political heavyweight. Others believe he may rise again if given the chance. But I wonder what legacy he will leave behind. He abandoned scholarship, contributed nothing of note to education and left no meaningful mark as a politician. He lived his life for himself alone. Honour and status were his ultimate goals. In the end, he did more harm than good to himself and to those around him.

I also know a woman who lost her husband during the Korean War. She managed his estate with great care and began work that she deemed meaningful. One of her efforts was rehabilitating women in the sex trade. She dedicated a portion of her inheritance to this cause. She didn't just oversee others doing the work, but invested her time and energy personally, as though she were a mother to each one of the women seeking help. She also donated a significant sum to a scholarship fund for underprivileged youth and asked that none of these acts be made public.

She had her reasons for giving up her life savings for the causes. She was in poor health and feared that anything could happen at any time. She left only a small amount of her wealth to her only daughter. 'Let's use the inheritance your father left us in a way that honours him and honours all of us,' she said to her daughter.

When I heard her story, I was deeply moved. Society has a duty to support marginalised people and work with them. But we have neglected that duty. If only more of us could live with such heartfelt concern for others, how much happier and more meaningful our society would become!

Offering Beauty and Receiving Respect

It was one late spring day when I was living in Boston, Massachusetts. Strong winds blew in from the Charles River, but it was not at all chilly.

Boston Symphony Orchestra is one of the finest orchestras in the United States. Professor H and I had gone out early in the day to get tickets for the last concert of the season, but tickets were sold out. As we passed Symphony Hall again later that day, its faded red-brick exterior struck me like the face of a lover who had spurned our advances. I couldn't help feeling a bit resentful.

But just as we were about to pass by the building, we were stopped in our tracks by a billboard that said that the night's programme was Beethoven's Ninth Symphony, conducted by Charles Munch in his farewell concert. We were so taken aback by this unexpected discovery that we could hardly speak. We felt like students who'd missed the application deadline for an exam.

Why hadn't we paid attention to the newspaper ads for the past few days? I was frustrated with myself. Of course, there were no tickets left at the box office. We tried pleading, but it was no use. Because this was Munch's farewell performance, tickets had been sold out days ago. We had no choice but to resign ourselves once again. Professor H, who had been in Boston longer than I had and had been looking forward to hearing the symphony, seemed especially downcast.

'Let's come back at admission time anyway,' he said to me. 'Who knows? Maybe someone who reserved a ticket won't show up?'

I agreed. There was always a chance we could get lucky.

As we wandered along the streets and dropped by a bookstore, the sun began to set. We had dinner at a Chinese restaurant, and when we looked at the clock, it was already twenty to eight. We headed back to Symphony Hall, standing near the entrance, watching the crowd. We went to the ticket window again and asked if there was any way we could get in.

The elderly clerk at the ticket office gave us an apologetic look.

'There are already dozens of people waiting just in case someone doesn't show up. You could join them, but I'm afraid it won't help.'

Sure enough, around two dozen people were waiting in line, but not a single reserved ticket was given up. Ticketholders were shown in, and soon the doors closed. We were like dogs staring longingly at a rooster that fled to the barn roof. We tried more begging and negotiating, but it was all in vain. About ten people gave up and left. Around twenty of us remained. One young man suggested that only a few of us should try negotiating while the rest waited out of sight, arguing that a big crowd might reduce our chances. Professor H and I ended up among those waiting by the side.

Soon the group returned, urging us all to go around to the back door. We sprinted to the back. We tried appealing to the doorman there too, but again, no success. We could already hear faint sounds of the orchestra through the doors. The concert had begun. All was lost.

Professor H and I exchanged disappointed looks, and people who were waiting in line dispersed one after another. As they left, several paused to exchange words of consolation with us. With everyone gone, we had no choice but to leave too.

'Well, let's go,' I said to Professor H.

'Being turned away twice like this, home feels about as far away as Seoul. Let's have a cigarette before we go.'

He slumped down on the stairs, very exhausted.

We had about a third of the cigarette left when an old man came up the stairs. Guessing from his uniform, he was a Symphony Hall staff. He was carrying a mop, a bucket and rags. He knocked on the locked glass door. An older doorman let him in, though the man struggled with all the tools in his arms.

Standing close by, I held the door for him and said with a smile, 'You're a lucky man.'

'Lucky? How's that?' he asked.

'We've been waiting all this time, trying to get in,' I said. 'But we couldn't get tickets.'

He chuckled and replied, 'Well, I'm sorry. But I won't be in there long, anyway.' Then he disappeared inside.

A few moments later, he re-emerged without the cleaning tools. I held the door for him again and, knowing nothing would come of it, asked anyway, 'There's just the two of us. Isn't there any way we could get in?'

He hesitated for a moment, then went back inside and spoke with two guards. A few minutes later, he returned and told me to go in and ask directly.

We quickly entered, thanked him profusely and explained our situation. Having come this far, we couldn't turn back. Eventually, they allowed us in for two dollars apiece and we were shown to the back of the third tier. It was standing room only, but that didn't matter.

From the highest point in the hall, we looked down. The space was packed, the stage full of orchestra and choir musicians. It felt like something out of a fairy tale, as if angels had taken their places onstage. Beethoven's majestic and powerful music filled the hall. It was as though the enraptured audience and ethereal music had come together to create a moment of pure beauty.

After each movement, thunderous applause shook the hall. The conductor had to bow again and again, but each time, he had the concertmaster or another performer take a bow with him, never seeking the spotlight for himself. This humility moved the audience even more.

Then the final movement began. The solo and choral parts were so sublime, they seemed to come not from the stage but from beyond the sea, beyond the sky. If heaven had music, surely it would sound like this.

For someone like me, who'd rarely had a chance to hear truly great music, it was beyond anything I'd imagined. The thousands in the audience held their breath. The moon and stars seemed to shine only for the stage. As the final chorus rang out, all of us present in the concert hall forgot ourselves, transported by ecstasy.

The concert came to an end. Applause and cheers erupted. They didn't stop. The conductor, Charles Munch, hesitated to return to the podium. When he did, he led the soloists out with him and recognised the concertmaster, directing all praise to the musicians.

After decades of working with them, each one must have felt like a dear friend to the conductor.

The applause only intensified. The audience rose in unison, urging Munch to take the podium once more. Finally, two or three performers led him up. The hall was about to burst with cheers and clapping. Bouquets were presented. After many bows, Munch left the stage. His humility and quiet dignity shone through. His silver hair made him seem like the embodiment of industry and dignity. I believe the applause went on for nearly half an hour before he exited the stage for the last time.

Following the crowds out of the concert hall in silence, I reflected on what we had just experienced. It had been a deeply, unimaginably moving experience. A conductor who had given the city the gift of music for decades was now stepping down as a silver-haired man. It was only natural that the citizens could not help but express both admiration and sorrow. How many concertgoers had been delighted by him during his tenure? How many young people had discovered music through him?

More than the music itself, what struck me most was the warmth of the citizens who cherished the conductor, and the deep affection the musicians clearly had for him.

Professor H seemed equally moved. We walked in silence for a long time.

As we were about to board the bus, I said, 'Boston really is a city worth living in.'

Professor H replied with something completely different: 'If I can have any say in it, I think I'd like to be a conductor in my next life.'

We both laughed. But our solemn expressions remained.

When I got home, it was already midnight. I lay down, but sleep wouldn't come. The melody of Beethoven's Ninth, the memory of Charles Munch's conducting, his humility, the ceaseless applause, the beauty of a city expressed through its music – all of it lingered in my heart.

PART THREE

A Loving and Joyful Heart

In youth, one is intoxicated with love for which one would give up life itself.
But with age comes wisdom, and wisdom changes the way we love.
Wise judgement, responsibility and the maturity of character
become more important than anything else in shaping a loving relationship.

Importance of Loving Wisely

Love and romance bring happiness and help us mature. Yet many people also become deeply unhappy because of love.

When I was young, I enjoyed reading Russian literature – Tolstoy and Dostoevsky, of course, but also the short stories of Anton Chekhov. Pushkin is often called the father of Russian literature. He was a poet and a pioneer, and *The Captain's Daughter* is among his most iconic works.

Pushkin died young at thirty-eight. I don't recall all the details, but as I remember it, his wife fell in love with an officer, and he ended up duelling him. He was shot and the wound contributed to his early death. At the time, society considered duelling a noble display of courage. But literary scholars still grieve the loss of the gifts Pushkin could have given to the world if his life had not been cut short. Duelling was common among aristocrats in Pushkin's day, but given his rational mind and religious convictions, the decision that led to his death was hardly in keeping with a life of wisdom.

Nowadays, no one fights duels over love. People no longer think of romantic affection as the whole of life. A love that demands one's life is considered outdated and incompatible with modern values.

But then again, this is perhaps not entirely true. You'll find no shortage of TV programme characters in their twenties and thirties who live as if love were everything. Men abandon work to pursue women, women who sacrifice everything in the name of love. Some even grow distant from their children or spouses as they pursue romantic interests.

How do these stories usually unfold? The characters choose a thorny path in the name of love, despite strong objections from family members and friends.

The other day, I overheard a delightful remark from an older woman engrossed in such a TV programme. 'They're still young, but they'll figure out eventually that they were playing with fire for no good reason. When you're our age, you realise love and hate don't matter. Jealousy is a young person's game.'

The woman was over seventy and struggling with health issues. In her eyes, the romantic squabbles of the young made good stories, but had nothing to do with her own life.

Years ago, there was a film that captivated viewers around the world: *Life Dances On*. The protagonist stumbles upon a dance card listing the names of her partners from a ball she attended in her youth. Curious, she sets out to find them. She tracks down seven of them, but all are now old and frail. The pleasures and beauty of youth are long gone. The film evokes the transience of life and reveals how our view of life evolves with age.

When we are young, we may be swept away by love. But as we grow older, the wisdom that age brings transforms the nature of love. Still, it would be dull if young people loved like the elderly. It may be ideal to love with youthful passion at first, then mature into a love that prioritises each other's happiness.

But if someone loves with reckless abandon into old age, it can be troublesome. I once knew of a gentleman who remarried at seventy-three and told his new wife, 'Do you know how much I cried because I feared our love might fall apart?' That kind of passion can seem admirable, but there's also something slightly unhealthy about it when it becomes all-consuming. He prioritised love over everything else and at the expense of all other relationships in his life. I remember feeling that way every time I saw him. I later heard that his children eventually lost respect for him. I would not condone their behaviour, either, but perhaps love in old age ought to be tempered by the wisdom that comes with it.

Strangely enough, those among my friends who once idolised romance and poured all their passion into love were the ones who often ended up divorced or unhappy at home. Those who married without grand passion or high expectations and instead worked to build family and stability tended to find quiet happiness and domestic contentment. Some might argue that one who has never been in love to begin with cannot fall out of love and dissolve a marriage. But if love bears fruit in the form of happiness, then perhaps the latter path makes more sense.

Taking a step back and looking at the big picture, subscribing to a few wise principles seems prudent.

First, there is more to love than romantic love. The Greeks distinguished between romantic love (*eros*) and friendship (*philia*) and later added religious love (*agape*). We need not just romantic love but also love for knowledge and art, and love for our neighbours and our country. If we understand this, we realise that romance is not all there is to life. Young people often lose balance in love because they fail to see the wholeness of what a relationship could and should be.

Second, true love should not be driven by emotion alone. It must be a love shaped by character. When young, we often make the mistake of believing that what we feel for the object of desire is the whole of love. It's often said that celebrities and artists have higher divorce rates. I can see why this might be the case. These individuals live rich emotional lives, but emotions are volatile, and sentiment can take unexpected turns. When love is fuelled more by emotion than reason, it is easily cooled, easily broken.

There's a well-known couple in our society, both famous artists. Because we were close, they once confided in me, 'If we hadn't had a Catholic wedding, we might have divorced long ago.' Artists tend to lead with emotion, and that alone is rarely enough. Without rational judgment and mature ideals, love can't last or grow in a healthy direction. This is why when famous people divorce, the usual culprit is 'incompatible personalities'. But more often than not, the root cause is a lack of rational thinking or maturity.

Third, love must include a broader purpose and vision. Love is not merely a private bond. It carries with it shared responsibilities, like raising children and nurturing a happy home. We also have a duty to our neighbours and society. From our homes may emerge future leaders who will shape the next generation. Participating in public service and contributing to society is also an important responsibility that we should all pay more attention to. This kind of love is a true and meaningful one that brings both happiness and honour.

When this kind of love becomes widespread, we gain the conviction that love can lead us towards a more fulfilling life and a happier society. Love in youth is beautiful. But love in old age, when marked by reverence, also has its grace. When both exist, we can offer the world the fruits of love.

*Imagine yourself on a stroll with Buddha
   at dusk listening to his teachings.
Or seated at a dinner table with Confucius,
   sharing a cup, taking in his generous character.
What kind of person am I? What kind of person
   would I like to be?*

Being a Good Friend

Just as each human face is different, so too are our personalities, social status and the respect we earn from younger generations.

It would, of course, be ideal to be both respected and likable. But sometimes, a person commands great respect while being, quite frankly, not all that pleasant to interact with. One might revere a person's academic or artistic accomplishments while feeling a distinct lack of affinity towards their personality. Imagine we could choose any historical figure as a close friend. How many can you think of that you would like to befriend? No matter how others might praise them, there are people whose ideas I admire but whom I would never want as a friend.

I loved Tolstoy deeply from a young age. At one point, I even shaped my entire worldview around his works. And yet, I never once thought I'd want him as a friend. His own inner contradictions, his perpetually furrowed brow as he tried to grapple with life's paradoxes might make him a figure worthy of admiration, but being his close companion would be difficult. He opposed consumption of meat but would sneak it at night. His extreme sense of piety driven by duty was less than ideal, and I suspect that the blind worship and respect he received likely made it hard for him to form friendships based on mutual fondness. Dostoevsky, on the other hand, might have been more approachable, even endearing, on a human level. Still, among Russian writers, the one I would most want to share close friendship with is Chekhov. His simple and unassuming nature and his ability to find beauty anywhere would have made him a good friend to anyone.

But some individuals, no matter how great, seem nearly impossible to befriend. Voltaire and Rousseau from the French Enlightenment, the father of social science Auguste Comte, Oliver Goldsmith who wrote *The Vicar of Wakefield*, America's brilliant Edgar Allan Poe, the pessimistic Schopenhauer, the human will-obsessed Nietzsche, Francis Bacon the philosopher of early modern England, Beethoven the saint of music, and Wagner the king of opera – these are some examples.

Their ideas and achievements were undoubtedly monumental, but it would be challenging, even painful, to be their lifelong friend. If there are a few who escape this category, Herbert Spencer and Strindberg may qualify. With a man like Nietzsche, I'd worry that he would either like me too much or too little. Wagner, for instance, was a figure who did not adequately appreciate young Nietzsche's admiration only to suffer from it later. Nietzsche's feelings for others ran in extremes – excessive admiration or bitter contempt. Thus, being the object of his respect never lasted long. He was the sort one was better off observing from afar.

Comte had a similar temperament. He couldn't govern his nature and suffered because of it. He fell in love with a vulgar woman and when the relationship failed, he tried to take his own life. He then worshipped a completely ordinary woman like an 'angel' just to find peace of mind.

I adore Beethoven's music. But if I had to live with him? That would be an unhappy life. Watching Beethoven in his old age bickering with his young cousin would hardly be pleasant. Rousseau would likewise not make a great companion. At age seven, when his teacher told him to stay behind after school for not doing his homework, he thought she was sending the others home to make advances on him. Later in life, he wept at being praised by noblewomen for a trivial composition. Being Rousseau's friend would be difficult, to say the least. Francis Bacon's arrogance and loquaciousness would hardly bring peace or joy to one's spirit. Schopenhauer had intoxicating ideas, but his arrogance, stubbornness and deeply warped worldview would be intolerable for most people.

Goethe is certainly worthy of the highest reverence. Yet his pride, his peculiar brand of individualism and the excessive praise showered on him would have made him unapproachable. Perhaps only someone like Johann Peter Eckermann could serve him with the sensitivity he required.

Some of the people I mentioned clearly suffered from deep psychological instability. We may be better off admiring their works from a distance.

Among musicians, Tchaikovsky might not make for an easy friend, but Chopin possibly could. Still, I'd worry he'd be too distracted by women to maintain a friendship. Byron's heroism doesn't feel so admirable either. Always seated on the throne in his own mind, he doesn't seem capable of giving his attention to one person for long. What about Kierkegaard? It would have been advisable for his friends to not meet him too often or say too much to him. He seems better suited for friendships with innocent children or gentle elders. If Regine Olsen had married him, she likely would have been burdened by his inexplicable spiritual turmoil.

There are, of course, great men in history capable of being anyone's friend despite their exceptional talent and the reverence they receive. Religious saints, for example, could be a good friend to all of humanity. Imagine going on an evening stroll through a village at the foot of a mountain, listening to the words of the

Buddha. Picture yourself seated around a table with Confucius, sharing a cup and basking in his welcome, wise presence. See yourself lying among the disciples under the olive trees of Gethsemane, listening to the voice of Christ and drifting into sleep. Surely these are the friends of the people.

Figures like Socrates, Saint Francis of Assisi, Kant and Mozart may not measure up to the religious saints but nevertheless seem like friends I'd want to have. After Socrates died, his disciples mourned him deeply, not only because of his philosophy or teachings, but his character, his warmth and his generosity. Saint Francis, a man of charity and humility, was called 'father' by his many followers. He would have been an unparalleled friend. Living with someone like Kant wouldn't feel awkward or uncomfortable. Imagine chatting with him each evening for half an hour after a day spent in thought and writing – what a delight! His sensitivity and gentle humanity, absent in thinkers like Hegel or Fichte, would be deeply appreciated. Among musicians, Mozart might have made the best companion. If I had to choose a travel companion for a month or two, I'd probably pick him.

Someone like Carl Hilty would be worth living with long-term and learning from his daily habits and convictions. He might have shared a lifestyle akin to that of Dr Albert Schweitzer.

Among Koreans I've met, I regret never having had a long friendship with people like Dosan Ahn Changho or Kim Seong-su. Of course, the age and generational gap would have been an obstacle.

What's curious, though, is that I've never felt drawn to befriend great political leaders or generals, no matter how much I searched. Kings, dictators and party leaders all seem to have lost the humility and warmth that make genuine friendship possible. Even worse are those who are arrogant, hypocritical educators, dogmatic scholars and artists-turned-politicians. These are the people I most wish to avoid. They make tiresome companions, impossible to find common ground with.

There are also people who are hard to approach because they're too passive. Some people never speak up, never express themselves, only ever watching for others' reactions. They mean no harm, yet their company feels joyless. It is likewise quite difficult to become friends with someone who only ever talks about themselves, regardless of who they're with. These people, excessively chatty with everyone they meet but gradually losing one friend after another. It's not necessarily bad to talk about oneself, but it's better to say too little than too much. It is also difficult to befriend someone with excessively strong and inflexible convictions. I believe that the beauty of a person's character grows in a gentle and generous heart. While strong beliefs can be admirable, it may be better not to express them too emphatically.

It is also quite challenging to deal with people who have carved out a position in society through relentless effort and hardship, if they keep reminding you of these efforts and hardships. Those who possess generosity of spirit and broad convictions are comforting to have around. They become like fathers, mothers or older siblings to us. But those who have built their lives on relentless toil and unceasing vigilance are often too mired in their problems, making them myopic and quick to judge. In my experience, this can lead to fatigue and unease in the relationship.

Teachers should treat every student with affection and pride, but there are always students who show little respect for their teachers' feelings. Some casually pry about a teacher's private life as though entitled, or seek favour by gossiping about their colleagues' shortcomings. Others might invest undue weight in a single comment that isn't worth meditating on and create reason to find awkwardness that doesn't need to be there.

Brilliant students and young, energetic scholars or artists whose work is beginning to gain recognition may take pride in their sharp intellect. But they would do well to remember Goethe's words: 'Wine, before it has fully matured and acquired its true flavour, foams and boils.'

What kind of person am I? What kind of person would I like to be?

Of course, not all of us will leave behind great achievements or earn widespread fame. But whether the difference is large or small, every one of us takes on our own personality. More than anything, we should cultivate a harmonious and well-rounded character. We must tend to our hearts and lives with a centredness that allows us to form meaningful connections with others.

We ought to abandon trivial fame, the unnecessary sense of superiority and the anxiety that comes from little emotional and spiritual wealth. Instead, we should strive to be free from narrow-mindedness. If such a way of life and attitude becomes widespread in society, then both our own happiness and the peace and dignity of humankind would be greatly enhanced.

Do unto others, as they say, as you would have them do unto you.

*Quality of life does not come from money or income.
What we truly need in life are
hobbies that aid our inner growth,
recreation that relieves fatigue, tension and stress,
and humour, a mark of those who don't take themselves too seriously.*

Three Gifts for a Satisfying Life

Years ago, a close colleague invited me to join him in a painting class every Sunday. I had to turn down his invitation as my schedule was not entirely free, and more importantly, I lacked any talent or aptitude for painting. Even in middle and high school, my art teachers had said they had never seen a student so poor at drawing. Perhaps it's genetic. My father, too, was famously unskilled with his hands.

That friend later became quite a good painter. His home and office were adorned with tasteful oil paintings he did, and I recall that he supported his daughter's studies abroad with the income he made from selling his art.

Instead of painting, I chose to write essays and reflections. I worried that the rigid logic of academic work might stunt my emotional growth, and thought a hobby might help. Fortunately, I had read widely when I was young and had been especially drawn to literature in school. My heart turned naturally in that direction. I wrote two essays a month to start out and had built up a modest collection before long.

During a summer break, the university newspaper reached out to a few professors who didn't usually contribute and asked us to write personal essays. I was chosen among the faculty of the College of Humanities. I submitted one essay I'd written some time ago to positive reception. In the fall, another essay was published. That opened the door for continued invitations from monthly and weekly publications.

In the end, about twenty of my essays were published. I added a few more and published them as a collection called *The Illness Called Loneliness*, which was well received. Soon after, a publisher requested another book. I was scheduled to spend a year in the United States and Europe that summer, so I wrote it quickly before I left. The result was *Dialogue Between Eternity and Love*. When I returned from my travels, I discovered that the book had attracted considerable interest, especially among younger readers.

To this day, many readers know me as an essayist rather than a philosophy professor. That wasn't my intention, but perhaps the warm and accessible essays reached a wider audience than my drier, perhaps more dense, philosophical writing.

Even if I'm not especially proud of my success as an essayist, I do believe the spiritual and emotional benefit I gained through the experience was immense. I was able to meet and converse with many readers, share a sense of purpose, and receive their gratitude. Some were even inspired to pursue philosophy further thanks to the essays.

My life as an essayist allowed me to take myself less seriously and gain emotional enrichment. This allowed me to grow more fully as a human being. Just as our bodies need a balance of nutrients to grow, our minds and souls also need nourishment. This is especially important for professionals whose work requires little to no emotional range. For them, taking up a hobby before they reach old age is incredibly valuable. Those who have experienced the benefits of a hobby understand that this is of no small importance.

A healthy and well-suited hobby can create more opportunities and a richer life. We sometimes see politicians who, trapped by self-interest and factionalism, fail to live by their own principles. Some people exhaust themselves chasing money from dawn till dusk as life passes them by. To such people, I would recommend expanding themselves through reading and getting in touch with a more emotional part of themselves through literature and the arts. Pursuing new avenues towards greater emotional intelligence is a wonderful way to begin a new chapter in life and discover new parts of oneself.

★ ★ ★

When asked what hobbies they have, some people mention sports or reading. But those aren't always true hobbies.

Jogging or swimming for the sake of health may be more of a duty than a hobby. One professor I know is what you'd call a baseball fanatic. He doesn't play the game himself, but is so preoccupied with it that he's become a kind of expert. He not only studies the stats and results of local games but keeps detailed notes on foreign players, too. His interest in Park Chan-ho bordered on professional research. That, I would say, is a genuine hobby.

Reading, in fact, isn't really a hobby for intellectuals but a duty. Academics tend to read for work, not leisure. But reading about medieval art, or a society's folk culture, for instance, can be a hobby. A hobby is more like a mental side-job – it's fun to consistently pursue something for pleasure.

Korean scholars in the pre-modern era enjoyed calligraphy. Scholars who weren't professional artists but still dabbled in art produced large volumes of amateur work, giving rise to the tradition of *muninhwa* – the scholar's painting. We can find traces of their influence in folk paintings.

Travelling or photography can be excellent hobbies. Appreciating music or fine art is another. I had a friend who had studied in Germany and, perhaps influenced by his time there, he developed a fondness for mechanics and fell in love with cars. He collected discarded parts and built his own vintage vehicles, which he enjoyed driving. That, too, is a hobby.

Sometimes, a person's hobby surpasses their profession. Perhaps Tolstoy first approached literature as a hobby while studying law. Tchaikovsky, too, began studying engineering before turning to music. Their times and society called for lawyers and engineers, but literature and music brought them joy and aligned with their talents. Ultimately, the hobbies they enjoyed became the paths through which they found success and served others.

There are many cases where a hobby ends up changing a person's career. And those who follow that path might even find greater success than if they had stuck to their original profession. When we do something because we love it, we don't tire as easily, and we awaken a deeper level of creativity within ourselves. Those who achieve fulfilling success are the ones who discover and develop their true self by looking into what's unique about them and finding their talents. And such people, surely, have lived the most satisfying lives.

But the kind of hobby I want to recommend here is not about hobbies that could develop into professional-level research or achievement. I encourage people who already have a job or career to also cultivate a personal interest to foster balance and growth outside of their day-to-day jobs.

A friend of mine, a physics professor, loved listening to classical music. He had a habit of spending an hour before bed every night simply listening. The results were remarkable. He could not only tell which performer was which by listening to the recordings, but also offer insightful commentary. His niece, a piano major, once asked him for feedback.

He once said, 'The most unfortunate person in the world is my wife. While I'm listening to my favourite pieces with all my focus, I turn to explain something to her – and she's fallen asleep! I don't know how she gets through life not appreciating such beautiful music.'

He often said that the greatest emotional richness in his life came not from physics, but from music appreciation.

My close friends generally avoid vices like gambling-related activities. They seem to believe such things neither enrich their emotional lives nor truly count as hobbies. A friend of mine dislikes games or hobbies that involve winning and losing. He believes that when you're fixated on the outcome, you miss the essence of the activity itself. The same applies to watching sports. If you're only watching to cheer for a team, you can't enjoy or objectively observe the game itself. The less invested you are in the outcome, the more you can simply enjoy the game and the moment for what it is.

A THEORY OF HAPPINESS

As for me, I've never really enjoyed activities like fishing, golf, hiking, go or *janggi* – that's not to say that you shouldn't find pleasure in these things. I found that I was always too busy to devote long hours to any one thing, not to mention I avoided games like *hwatu* because I disliked anything that made my head feel heavy. Thinking was my profession, so I didn't want to overwork my mind in my leisure time.

In the past few decades, however, I've developed an appreciation for traditional Korean ceramics and folk paintings. Whenever I felt tired or had a bit of free time, I'd visit museums and galleries. Browsing antique stores in Insadong brought me great joy as well. From that came a sense of aesthetic appreciation, a deeper sense of national pride, and above all, a love of our cultural heritage that became a spiritual asset for me.

As people grow older, they inevitably become lonelier and are pushed off the stage of professional life. Their field of work demands ever fiercer competition, and eventually, one must yield the spotlight to the next generation. In this transitional period in life, if you're able to devote yourself to a hobby you've cherished, it can offer a great deal of happiness and provide a meaningful sense of purpose.

One senior professor I knew had spent his entire life in academia. After retirement, he started going to his son's house every morning to read and study, and returned home at five to devote himself to growing orchids. The income he earned from cultivating orchids was nearly equivalent to his monthly salary when he was teaching. He kept up that routine until he passed away at eighty-six. Investing time in a skill and hobby like this is a good example of the retirement years well spent.

Those who work a lot often find that it's more efficient to switch between different tasks rather than sticking to just one until they are exhausted. Instead of resting after exercise, reading a book or writing something can be more productive. Physical fatigue can be relieved by mental activity, and mental stress by physical exertion. This is often more effective than resting by doing nothing at all.

Life follows a similar principle. It's ideal for those in mentally taxing professions to have physically active hobbies, and for those in physically demanding jobs to pursue intellectual ones.

On a visit to Northern Europe some years ago, I met a young couple living a very satisfying life. The husband worked in a factory as a skilled labourer but spent weekends in the park painting with his wife and two young children. He'd loved art in high school, and now he was reclaiming that passion. His wife took a literature course at a university for two hours a week and considered it a form of intellectual cultivation beyond her responsibilities at home. Their two children walked between them, enjoying the time outdoors.

This reminded me that a fulfilling life doesn't depend on wealth but on hobbies that foster inner growth and connection to the places and people around us.

There are areas of overlap between hobbies and entertainment. A form of entertainment that one has enjoyed for years may become a hobby, and a hobby one casually dips into may amount to mere entertainment. Entertainment doesn't require depth or effort and is meant to be enjoyed in brief moments. Yet even this kind of leisure can relieve fatigue and stress from work. That's why, especially for people in urban environments, entertainment is essential and we should carve out time to enjoy it.

Sometimes, the same activity can feel like either a hobby or entertainment depending on the approach. Watching a movie mindlessly and forgetting about it is entertainment. But reflecting on a film's deeper layers makes it a hobby. When entertainment evolves and gains depth, it becomes a hobby. And when a hobby becomes irregular and not very engaging, it often turns into entertainment. This isn't to say that entertainment is inferior or lacks value compared to hobbies. Entertainment rejuvenates some people, while others find joy in their hobbies. But if we must pick one or the other, devoting ourselves to one or two lasting hobbies may be more conducive to finding fulfilment over a lifetime than indulging in too many forms of entertainment.

Ideally, a variety of hobbies and entertainments is best. It's unwise to belittle someone else's interests or to judge them based on rigid moral standards. There was once an educator who disapproved of golf, thinking it a frivolous bourgeois hobby in a poor country like ours. He often told his juniors so. But in his later years, as a treatment for diabetes, he began playing golf himself. The health benefits and mental peace he gained from it were enormous. From then on, he began recommending golf to his juniors. While golf has become more popular in Korea today, in places like the United States it was never considered to be a middle-class sport to begin with. If one is willing, it can be enjoyed without much expense, and often quite close to home. One university in Japan even built a golf course to help fund school operations.

All hobbies and entertainments are a matter of personal choice. The only condition that matters is that the pastime does not bring harm to the world. Casinos, for instance, are universally popular. The more affluent and risk-prone a society, the more casinos tend to flourish. Korea is heading in this direction. I've heard there's a casino in Gangwon-do where Korean nationals can legally gamble. I wouldn't claim that casino games are categorically wrong, but when such entertainment becomes a hobby, and then a full-blown vocation, it veers into the realm of gambling. There are more wholesome and productive hobbies out there. Devoting one's life to entertainment that society can't respect is not recommended.

Finally, let's consider entertainment's power to create things anew. 'Recreation' is 're-creation', Entertainment can release us from fatigue, tension and stress, and enable us to engage in higher pursuits. In that way, it becomes more than a hobby but a necessity for modern life.

And because entertainment is often enjoyed with others, it strengthens our social bonds and fosters goodwill. This is one reason we're seeing more entertainment spaces appear around us – they provide another means to connect with each other.

Outside of hobbies and entertainment, there's one more way to lift the spirit: humour.

Years ago, I visited Dr Frank Schofield, a Canadian veterinarian working in Korea. He said to me, 'Everyone else is offering me condolences, but not you, Mr Kim?'

I asked, 'Did something happen recently?'

He replied, 'My younger brother died.'

I said, 'I'm sorry. I didn't know you had a younger brother?'

He answered, 'Didn't you see the paper yesterday? My brother in Changgyeongwon died.' Then he laughed. I laughed too. Dr Schofield's nickname was 'Tiger Grandfather', and the tiger at Changgyeongwon Zoo had died the day before.

I added, 'I feel bad now – I've only met you in your office, never at the zoo. Did you skip dinner last night out of grief?'

He said, 'I ate last night. As for today, I'll have to think about it,' and laughed again.

When I was in middle and high school in Pyongyang, Professors Yang Ju-dong and Chae Pil-geun of Soongsil School were the intellectual giants of their day. The two once served as judges at a speech contest.

To announce the winners, Professor Yang gave his comments and stepped down. Professor Chae took the podium and said, 'Professor Yang is the better judge for such events. He has two mouths (*yang* meaning 'two', *ju-dong* a near homonym for 'mouth'), so he speaks well. I only have one, so I can't say much.' Everyone laughed, and the stuffy atmosphere relaxed instantly.

There's also the famous Mr Ryu. In a group gathering, he asked his friend Reverend Kang, who is also quite famous, 'May I ask what clan you're from?' Reverend Kang replied, 'I'm from the Jinju Kang clan.' Everyone was curious why he wanted to know.

Mr Ryu said, 'Ah, I see! I asked because our new puppy (*kang-aji*) is from Jinju too, so I wondered if you might be from the same clan.'

Everyone around burst into laughter. Mr Ryu is known for such witty jokes, and he brings laughter wherever he goes. Perhaps that's why he remains healthy and active even in old age. Someone once joked, 'He'll live past one hundred. People grow old after they mature, but since he's never lost his juvenile sense of humour, he'll live forever!'

Unfortunately, humour is disappearing from our lives. There's too much tension and fighting, and no room for levity. The rhetoric of our political spokespeople is coarse and embarrassing. It may take decades before Korean politicians can use humour.

The Anglo-Saxons, particularly the British, are perhaps the most masterful at using humour. They enjoy witty remarks both in private and in public.

Humour isn't a hobby or entertainment, but it serves a vital psychological function, easing fatigue and tension. In today's stressful world, humour can be just as valuable as entertainment. It's the natural resting pulse of those who are both emotionally grounded and mature, and a welcome gift of the heart.

How noble is a life lived to the fullest through scholarship and hobbies!

A Meaningful Life

In the summer of 1974, I visited renowned physicist Professor Honk of Freiburg University with a Korean student. His modest, quiet home was tucked away in a forest, but what caught my eye was the elegant, classically styled furniture that was immaculately arranged in every room. It felt like the home of an artist rather than a physicist, or one furnished by a professional interior designer.

Some time later, I learned through the student who accompanied me that Professor Honk was originally from the Netherlands. It was his boyhood dream to become a fine cabinetmaker. He loved furniture from an early age and passionately hoped to devote his life to the craft.

But then, misfortune struck in his youth. He was afflicted with a severe case of polio. Though he survived, he was left physically disabled. He lost function in one arm, and he walked with a slight limp. The prolonged illness also left his physical strength greatly diminished. With his body no longer capable of handling strenuous manual labour, he had no choice but to give up his dream of becoming a furniture maker. His family encouraged him to chart a new path, and after much thought, he resolved to devote himself to study and become a scientist. He ultimately chose theoretical physics.

He later married a woman dedicated to social work and led a scholarly life in their modest home. But he never gave up on his childhood passion. With the help of his family, he crafted much of the furniture around the house himself. He created beautiful, unique pieces that could be found nowhere else. He set up a shop in the basement, and despite his physical limitations, he continued to make furniture with his own hands.

His unassuming and joyful devotion to a fulfilling career and hobby gave his life meaning. Perhaps this is what it truly means to live a worthwhile life.

Just as machinery breaks down if not properly greased, rest is necessary to accomplish greater work. When leisure disappears from our lives, life's richest rewards elude us.

Recovering the Sense of Leisure

Our modern age is often called the era of mechanism. Functionalism has become the standard of life, and we live in an age where machines reign supreme. Remove science and mechanism from modern society, and the entire system would come to a halt. Today's reality is one in which technology and machinery have come to dominate everything.

The overwhelming majority of people have left rural areas for cities, and urban life now operates entirely within mechanical rhythms. It is no longer possible to live in the city without machines. Our economy has also shifted to mechanised production and consumption. As these trends intensify, life becomes more convenient and abundant.

But therein lies the problem. In the midst of these transformations, we have lost touch with nature, surrendered room to breathe and become emotionally depleted. In short, we have lost emotional space.

Workers labour all day with machines as though they are extensions of those machines. Managers and salespeople run tirelessly through rigid, time-pressed routines. Those in leadership positions are in back-to-back meetings all day. We now know how to work efficiently, but not how to live. It's been a long time since we even had the mental space to ask what the meaning or purpose of life might be. Of course, there are people who try not to live this way but even they, to some extent, are eventually swallowed up by the same reality.

I once read an article about a Korean writer who returned from a trip to the United States shocked that American writers used typewriters to draft their manuscripts. In a time when Korean writers wrote longhand, the idea of writing a novel or composing a poem on a typewriter was unimaginable to him. We cannot avoid the fact that modern life requires us to embrace the help and advantages of machines.

I do not believe these social changes are wholly wrong. But if our lives become too one-sided, we risk incurring irreversible misfortune. Life must always seek balance, and history must always walk the path of integrity. So then, what attitude and direction must we adopt in this modern reality?

To put it simply, we must recover a sense of leisure. Just as machinery breaks down if not properly greased, rest is necessary to accomplish greater work and to live fully. When leisure disappears from our lives, life's richest rewards elude us.

★ ★ ★

How, then, do we recover the sense of leisure?

First, modern people must make more time to reconnect with nature. One of the chronic illnesses of our age is the destruction of nature as we simultaneously claim to miss the forests and rivers we've destroyed. The growing number of city dwellers who seek rural homes or vacation spots proves the point. Nature is our mother. It is humanity's original home. We are born with the destiny of returning to the earth from which we came. For that reason, we must love, care for and live in harmony with nature. Green spaces ought to surround factories. Office buildings should have views of forests and parks. In Europe, ideal city planning has created towns where farms and apartments coexist. The closer human life is to nature, the more happiness and inner calm it brings.

Second, we must separate work and private life. Some people tend to personal matters at work or bring work home. Doing private work at your job blurs these boundaries, and so does never quite getting off the clock. We must strive for balance and a healthy separation between the two so that we can thrive in both areas.

In other countries, professors typically conduct research at their universities and keep their private lives at home. They arrive early to campus, devote themselves to lectures and research, and return home in the evening to spend time with family and pursue their hobbies. Because of this balance, they can maintain their academic pursuits for a lifetime without overworking themselves mentally and physically. This is also why many professors abroad don't keep books at home and instead save their home spaces for their leisure activities. They believe greater achievements require inner calm, and that creative work is sustained by mental rest. If something urgent arises, they simply return to the office to take care of it, then go home. This separation of space in their daily routine is one of the ways they create psychological balance. Perhaps we, too, should consider this approach in order to recover mental and emotional space.

Third, we must cultivate inner leisure through reading, the arts and other forms of enrichment. In our times, everyone should strive to be both intelligent and cultured. An intelligent person is one who reads and reflects. A cultured person is someone who enjoys cultural heritage and participates in cultural activities. But it's not being seen as an 'intellectual' or 'cultured person' that matters. Those who read and reflect can view events and objects through an objective lens, which offers them perspective. Those who engage with culture and enjoy it tend to be more well-rounded and interesting individuals.

If you haven't read even a single book all year, or taken the time to organise your thoughts on any issue, how can you possibly have mental or emotional room to breathe? We are surrounded by cultural artifacts, museums and treasures that are cherished and praised by many. It would indeed be a harsh, impoverished life if one never took the opportunity to enjoy them. Of course, the deeper one's engagement with culture, the more they reap from this engagement. Over time, they cultivate deeper insight and connection to the world around them. Whether you are a novice or a connoisseur, these are paths anyone can access.

Isn't it wonderful when someone who has struggled with machines all day can enjoy a short essay or poem in the evening? Or when someone who's spent all day meeting others can, at night, gaze at a great painting or immerse their soul in a work of art? And yet, so many of us ignore the cultural wealth readily available to us. Perhaps we assume we are unworthy of such a life, denying ourselves such treats. But a life without time to read or opportunity and space to absorb or exchange intellectual nourishment is no life at all.

Finally, to recover mental space, we must ensure that we make the time to lose ourselves in joy. Through recreation and finding the fun in life, we release stress. In order to begin anew or create something fresh, we need time to relax our minds. For people today, nothing is more vital than releasing mental strain and psychological pressure by leaning into the truly joyous moments in life.

We must strive to grow by being kind to one another, and reflect on who we are so that we may live more purposeful lives. In that sense, our character grows alongside our work, and our work yields better results when we learn to take a step back and bring fresh perspectives to it through rest. This is why we must treat our leisure and downtime as an essential source of wisdom.

PART FOUR

The Road to the Completion of Life

*From negation to affirmation,
from anxiety to trust, from despair to hope,
from loss to actualisation –
this is our calling, our will.
And the duty to give it our sincere effort
has been entrusted to us.*

What Fills My Being

'I looked around. There was no one there. I began to feel uneasy.'

This line appears in the *Upanishads*, the ancient Indian philosophical text. Blaise Pascal confessed, 'I am terrified by the infinite vastness of space.'

The silence of the space surrounding me brings at times unease and at other times fear. If that silence were eternal, I don't think I could go on living because of the loneliness it would bring. If space were truly infinite, I feel I would not be able to preserve myself in the face of that infinity. The loneliness of silence and the anxiety induced by the infinite seem poised to swallow me whole.

Can't I simply consider myself part of that silence? Reduce myself to a speck in the vastness – would that not be enough?

But no, I cannot do that. If I were to bury my will and thoughts in silence, to let myself fall into eternal slumber within infinity, that would mean the loss of my imagination, the loss of my world and universe.

No matter how small and insignificant I may be, like a mayfly living only a day, my consciousness and awareness are in and of themselves a reality equal in weight to the universe. Even if I am anxious, it is I who feel that anxiety in relation to the world. If I tremble in fear, it is I who faces off against the universe.

Though I long to conquer and possess the world that surrounds me and to make it a place of peace and comfort, I find myself being penetrated and overpowered by the boundless space. Like someone stranded in a desert in a raging storm, desperately needing to pitch a tent for shelter, I feel I must cling to what little flicker of life I still possess within the silence and the infinity that stares back at me.

Even as I know full well that the finite is nothing within the infinite... I find myself unable to let go. In a sense, my life feels like a battle I cannot win, yet cannot walk away from. How absurd, for a creature no more than five feet tall to challenge the vast, infinite universe! And yet, I believe that it is my duty to fight it to the end.

I can remember one evening when my mother said again that she wished to return to her hometown. It had been thirty-six years since the Korean War drove her from it, and not a single day had passed without her speaking of that place.

'I wonder who lives in our house now...'

'When autumn comes, do the chestnut trees still drop their fruit in the yard as they used to?'

'Is the old wardrobe, passed down from my grandmother, still sitting in the lower room?'

'Who's keeping the silver spoons I brought with me when I married?'

These are the stories she told, and it was because of the memories that she said she longed to return. We tried gently to dissuade her. We reminded her that there was more for her in Seoul, and that the dream of returning to her hometown was one that may not happen for years. But her reply was always simple: 'Still, I must return to my hometown before I die.'

To my mother, her hometown was the place she was devoted to, where her body and her life dwelled. That was where she longed to be when she lay herself down for the final time. Perhaps this is what it means to be human: to carry, all our lives, a longing for familiar places and beloved spaces and return to where our heart once felt at home.

My friend C often says, 'Someday I must go back to the banks of the Charles River where my most beautiful dreams were born.'

C lost his beloved wife a few years ago. And whenever he misses her, he seems unable to forget the river where they first met, where their love was nurtured in the early months of the relationship. He keeps saying he must visit the river on the other side of the world once more before he dies.

We humans become attached to many places over the course of our lives, only to lose them and eventually drift away ourselves. In the end, we try to hold onto many spaces, but we cannot take any of them with us. We are wanderers with no true home. Strangers who came from somewhere unknown and will return to who knows where.

Like birds nesting in trees, we build our homes on the earth. Birds, though they fly thousands of miles, find peace only when they return to their nest. We too find rest only when we return to our own room, our own house, no matter how far we've travelled, to the place we believe is ours. This longing for space – for a home, for belonging – seems to be what propels our lives.

Some years ago, I had two of my front teeth pulled at the dentist. It left me more heartsick than I expected. When I came home and showed my teeth to the family, I received a range of responses.

'It happens. We all lose things as we age,' said my mother.

'You should take better care of your teeth from now on. Some people manage to keep their teeth all their lives, you know,' said my wife.

'You don't look like yourself anymore, without your front teeth,' said my daughter.

'I should have taken one more look at your face before you went to the dentist, Grandpa,' said my grade-school-aged grandchild.

I looked again in the mirror. I felt as if I had lost an important part of myself. Little by little, I will keep losing these parts until I lose my entire body. That will be the day I die. Death, after all, is the moment when we lose the space we call 'me'.

In that sense, one's body is the most important of all spaces. It isn't just my space, but my being itself. The loss of space is the loss of the body, and the loss of the body is the loss of self and the life it was connected to. In an attempt to cope with this loss at the end of everyone's road, or perhaps to escape it however we can, we have created art, philosophy and religion. But fact is fact. The time will come when we must part from everything we've loved – the sky, the sea, the mountains, the forest paths, the flowers, the birds, the stars, the moon, our neighbours, our homes, our families, our friends and even our own bodies – the space that was 'me'.

When we think about it, life is a solitary journey that begins and ends alone. That is why Heidegger referred to humans as 'thrown beings'. No one knows who threw us, so there is no one to hold accountable. All we know is that we find ourselves already thrown into existence. As such, endless anxiety and concern dominate us. We cannot return to where we were thrown from. Nor do we have refuge in which to seek peace. In the modern age, we are all wanderers who have lost homes to return to.

So, what are we to do? We must search for the home we've lost. We must create a place where we can be at peace. That is our fundamental task and our earthly mandate. But how could such a thing be possible?

Let's shift our thinking for a moment.

Are we truly beings thrown into existence with no purpose or meaning? Are we like pumpkins falling from the sky, dropped without intention or reason?

Let's assume that were true. Still, I was raised by parents who loved me dearly. I had siblings who supported me no matter what. There were kind neighbours who doted on me and friends who shared deep bonds and sustained that love over time. In my life, I've had people who loved me without conditions, who remained with me to the very end of life's journey. If I had treated them with more thought and sensitivity to their needs, we would have been even closer, and the depth of that affection would have stayed with me forever. Given the experience I've had, it seems more accurate to say that I am not a 'thrown being', but a 'given being' — a being entrusted with something.

Let's further expand on this idea.

The clear, blue sky. The ebb and flow of the vast sea. The hush of a lush forest. Stars that shine from different corners of the night sky. Plants that flower and bear fruit. Tender-hearted friends who offer empathy. Lovers who share profound love. The songs of birds echoing across quiet mountains and rivers…

Is this not the very joy of life, the reward of being alive, the beauty that brings happiness? Those who complain and speak only of unhappiness despite what the world offers may be too selfish and too narrow-minded to grasp the order of nature and the universe. Like a child who receives a dollar while others receive quarters and yet complains he did not receive a ten-dollar bill, they are caught in the misery of insatiable greed. They foolishly curse life simply because they cannot bend the universe to their will.

Considering all that we are given in life, human beings are not 'thrown' into being. We are, I would go so far as to say, chosen. Blessed. There are many who share this view.

If so, the issue lies not in the world around me, nor in the infinity of the universe, but in how I perceive it. My view, my interpretation, my stance, is what matters.

We humans can look at the same thing with joy or sorrow. We can face a single truth with either pain or delight. Some mourn their greying hair, while others wear it as a crown of glory. Some collapse beneath life's burdens, while others overcome suffering to recover the ecstasy of living.

The question is, which of these paths are we on?

One person sees the world and the infinite as a hostile, demonic force that devours them. Another sees the same world as a gift, an embrace of benevolence, given for their sake. Which one am I?

That is the question each of us must answer. To move from negativity to positivity, from anxiety to trust, from despair to hope, from loss to actualisation — this is our task and calling. Our ancestors walked this path. The wise worked towards this fulfilment. And now, it is our responsibility to inherit their hard-earned wisdom.

And may the boundless infinity of space be filled with your truth, your beauty, your goodness.

A Slightly Melancholy Story

I heard something from my friend, a senior professor, a few years ago that has stayed with me.

'Mr Kim, I've been thinking about what it really means to grow old. One thought that keeps returning is that aging is the gradual shrinking of one's world. When I was still at the university, I didn't feel the need for a retirement festschrift. But it was something everyone else was doing, and the junior professors put a great deal of work into it, so I accepted it gratefully. Once the publication was covered in the papers and became known to the public, everyone suddenly began to treat me like an old man. I hadn't changed, but others now saw me differently.

'Even the greetings began to change. People who used to make casual observations like, "You're in early today," or simply, "Good morning," were now asking, "Are you keeping well these days?" or "How are you passing the time lately?" They were subtly pushing me out of their realm of activity, even though there was nothing wrong with me. So in the five years that remained between my sixtieth birthday and retirement, I hardly got any research done and simply waited for my time to be up.

'Then I officially retired. My world shrank and my work disappeared. In other words, my professional space vanished, and my sphere of life was reduced to the home. I suppose I really started aging at sixty, but by sixty-five, the thought that I am really "elderly" began to weigh on me.

'These days, I even feel somewhat alienated at home. Of course, the house is mine, so who can object to me being there? But still, I can't help noticing certain things. Until my fifties – and even into my sixties – every time I was late coming home, my wife would ask where I'd been, who I'd met and joke about whether I'd been seeing "the other woman" again. But after I turned sixty, she no longer cared. Now, when I come home, she seems almost disappointed. She asks, "Back already? Don't you have anywhere to go?"

'She suggested, "Why don't you go out more often?"

'I'd love to!' my friend retorted. 'But I haven't got the money. My secret stash has dried up.' So he joked back about 'the other women' who were dying to see him, but his wife knew he had nowhere to go and no one to see. One day, his daughter-in-law quietly slipped him a 10,000-won bill and suggested he go out for a bit. 'So that's why I'm out today,' he said to

A THEORY OF HAPPINESS

me, recounting the story. He admitted that without realising it, his space at home has started to shrink too. 'And where else is there to go anymore besides my plot in the cemetery?'

I began to feel sad listening to him. It struck me that perhaps life is the process of expanding one's sphere, only to be gradually pushed out of it until one disappears entirely from the public realm.

I've followed a similar trajectory as well. Compared to many, my social sphere was relatively wide. In the 1960s, I spent time in the United States and even travelled around the world twice. I was incredibly lucky. I sometimes visited my three daughters who lived in the States and I often gave lectures in North American cities for Korean expats. I spent most winter and summer breaks abroad. I took many personal trips as well. Once, when I was boarding a flight in Australia bound for Seoul, a Korean Air representative greeted me and said, 'Thank you for flying with us so frequently.' It turned out that was my 900th Korean Air flight. And I flew with many other airlines as well. That's how much I travelled and how expansive my social space had been.

But starting in the mid-1990s, my world began to shrink. As I aged, my work responsibilities were cut back, and there were fewer places to go. In time, long trips became a burden for me. Some hotels even began to express concern, asking, 'Will it be all right for an elderly person to stay alone?'

I stopped making frequent trips abroad. I still receive occasional invitations to speak in regions outside the capital, but most of my engagements now are within Seoul so that I don't have to travel such long distances.

For twenty years since retirement, I've been going to a gym on Namsan and frequented hotel cafés, like the one at the Hyatt. For health, I would swim a little, and while sipping coffee, I'd jot down outlines for lectures or manuscripts. It was more efficient and less tiring to rest at a café after a talk in Gangnam than to go all the way back home to Sinchon, only to head out again.

But for the past two or three years, even those lectures have dwindled. Now I spend more days resting at home than giving talks. Soon, I might end up living a life where I only work every other day. That's why I recently began using public transportation. Since most of my time is now spent in consumption rather than production, I felt it fitting. But even that isn't easy – subways have bad air quality and give me headaches, and buses feel unsafe. Too often I sense other passengers looking at me as if to say, 'Old folks should just stay home rather than take up seats on public transportation.'

So, this summer, I plan to stop going to the Namsan gym and instead swim at a nearby facility. I only swim about 200 metres at a time, but I still want to keep it up for a few more years.

As I made up my mind to change where I went for my swims, I realised I'd probably go to downtown Seoul less and less. My daily orbit would shrink to the Yeonhui-dong–Sinchon area. If I had errands, I could walk to Sinchon Rotary, maybe take the village bus or enjoy a short stroll. That would be my life's remaining sphere.

Two years ago, my children worried that the stairs from the front gate to the main entrance and the stairs from the first to the second floor would become too dangerous for me to navigate, so they had safety rails installed. Eventually, I will need those handrails to get in and out of the house and up and down from the living room to my upstairs study.

Still, I'm thankful. I have friends who, because of severe arthritis or injuries, are confined to their rooms. I'm grateful things aren't worse for me – yet. But of course, those situations aren't entirely someone else's story. If the stairs become too hard to climb, I'll have to move my bedroom downstairs.

My mother passed away in the small room downstairs. My wife had passed away before that in the master bedroom. My mother, who used a cane, moved between the living room and her room, but my wife, who had been bedridden for a long time, couldn't leave the master bedroom. Eventually, when even the wheelchair could no longer carry her past the bedroom doorway, she closed her eyes for good.

I'll likely end up the same way, though I don't wish it. That's the fate that awaits. That's how the physical space of my life will eventually come to an end.

From this perspective, what the senior professor said is an inevitable truth for everyone. It is, indeed, a slightly sad thing to think about.

But a person's life is not confined to physical space, nor does it end there.

What matters more is the space occupied by meaning. Physical space is temporally limited as well, but the field of meaning we carry within is not. Quality trumps quantity.

Alexander the Great conquered and ruled more territory than anyone. But his spiritual legacy is hard to trace. In contrast, his tutor, Aristotle, possessed very little physical space – his library in Athens, the tree-lined walks with his students. He did not speak in grand lecture halls. Yet his intellectual legacy has shaped the past 3,000 years and continues to offer philosophical truth to the world.

Among those who lived in the narrowest of physical spaces was the philosopher Kant. Born in the small German town of Königsberg (now Kaliningrad, Russia), he lived, studied and taught there his entire life. It's said he never left his hometown. Aside from regular walks, he spent all his time in his university office and classroom. In retirement, his entire life was confined to his study and the path he used for daily walks. But the philosophy he produced there became the shared inheritance of all humanity. From the smallest space, he carved out one of the vastest domains of intellectual life.

So, in the end, life is not determined by how large or small our physical sphere is. What matters is what we leave behind in that space. Life, I now believe, is about inscribing infinite meaning within a finite frame.

Friendships in the Twilight Years

In early summer of 1962, I boarded a flight from New York to London with my longtime friends, Professor Ahn Byung-wook and Professor Han Woo-geun of Seoul National University's history department.

Professor Han had just completed a year of research at the Harvard-Yenching Institute in Cambridge, Massachusetts, and Professor Ahn and I were scheduled to stay in the United States for a year as visiting professors at the invitation of the U.S. State Department.

Having spent a semester together at Harvard, Professor Han and I had built a deep and easy friendship, bonding over the solitude of life abroad. My friendship with Professor Ahn went even further back.

At that time, travelling around Europe or circling the globe wasn't easy. Fortunately, our travel and living expenses were fully covered by the United States, allowing us to plan a long trip without financial strain.

The three of us, like students preparing for a school trip, laid out a detailed itinerary and visited universities, cultural landmarks and art museums across Europe. In the evenings, we returned to our hotel rooms and exchanged our thoughts on what we saw that day, often weaving together historical and philosophical reflections.

It was a joyful, deeply fulfilling journey. The cultural riches of Britain, Germany, France, Switzerland and Italy left us dazzled, while the historical legacies of Athens and Cairo elevated our intellectual awareness.

Once we returned to Seoul, however, the three of us did not have a chance to gather again. We each became busy, and Professor Han's field of research diverged from ours. Decades would pass before we would gather again.

Then, in the summer of 1997, I heard through several friends that Professor Ahn was suffering from chronic bronchitis. While not life-threatening, battling an illness would still be hard on a man approaching eighty. After years of teaching and giving lectures, having to limit or stop his work altogether would have been a loss for him and his field.

After a couple of days contacting Seoul National University and other acquaintances, I finally tracked down Professor Han's address and phone number. I wanted to talk about old times, cheer him up, and perhaps reunite the three of us. Professor Ahn was living in an apartment near Walkerhill Hotel, so we arranged to meet at the café in the lobby. It was late autumn of 1997, thirty-five years since we had last all been together.

That day, it felt as if we had all returned to our forties. Our conversation flowed endlessly, one story leading to the next. The view of the Han River from the hotel café reminded us of the Daedong River in Pyongyang, where all three of us had spent our middle- and high-school years. We were so absorbed in our reunion that the two hours we planned for coffee went by in a flash. We promised to meet four times a year, with the changing of each season. Post-IMF crisis, we all had a bit more free time, and three months between visits suddenly felt too long.

Anyone overhearing our conversation that day would not just have been curious, but astonished. The three of us chatted like travellers in our forties discussing sights we'd just seen, not old men in our eighties reminiscing. Professor Ahn would glance around the café and ask, 'No one's listening, right?' before launching into stories. We listened with bright eyes and burst into laughter time and again.

At one point, a hotel staff member approached us with a smile and said, 'Watching you three talk and laugh together – you look like teenage boys. What are you talking about that's so funny?'

We continued to gather at the Walkerhill café every three months or so and made such an impression that the staff recognised us. When one of us arrived first and stepped away, they'd let the others know, 'Professor So-and-so was here and just went to the restroom.' They seemed genuinely intrigued that old men could be so excited and happy to get together.

Our cheerful gatherings continued for two years, with the support and delight of our wives. We imagined we'd continue meeting this way for a long time. Over time, Professor Ahn's health even began to improve.

Our last meeting was on Monday, 6 September, 1999. As we parted, we said, 'Next time will be our final meeting of the twentieth century. After that, it'll be a new millennium!' We were thrilled at the thought.

On the way home, Professor Han told us he was preparing to present to younger historians about the early days of the Korean Historical Association. He said that our get-togethers made him feel as if he were back in his forties, full of energy and joy. As we parted, he gave his usual awkward smile and waved his right hand gently. I got into the car and waved back, 'See you in December.'

But fate did not honour the wishes of three aging friends. On the morning of 29 September, as I flipped through the newspaper, I saw a photo of Professor Han. It was an obituary about the passing of a distinguished historian. In shock, I immediately called

Professor Ahn, who had just returned from his morning walk. He, too, was speechless. In our hearts, we both thought, *If only he could have lived to see the year 2000.* Our little gatherings stopped. Neither Professor Ahn nor I could bring ourselves to meet again. The memory of Professor Han loomed too large.

As time passed and we entered the twenty-first century, the sense of renewal seemed to offer a kind of emotional reset. It was a time of new beginnings in many ways.

Though our trio had disbanded, I began to wonder if another kind of gathering might be possible. Professor Han was gone, but those of us left behind still needed the occasional infusion of verve to keep us going.

A friend who came to mind immediately was Professor Kim Tae-gil of Seoul National University's philosophy department. People often referred to the three of us – Professor Kim, Professor Ahn and myself – as the 'Three Musketeers of Philosophy', because we were similar in age, field and professional activity. Professor Kim had devoted himself more to academic pursuits, while Professor Ahn stood out in the public sphere, but we were all playing on the same field.

I had been toying with the idea of bringing us three together. Then, during a phone call about another matter, Professor Ahn suggested Professor Kim first.

He said he hadn't realised until recently how meaningful the number three could be. While we had lost one member of the old trio, perhaps a new three could be formed. I told him I'd been thinking the same. He added that it might carry a new, more intellectually rich dynamic – more philosophical, more academic. And, he said, sharing face-to-face conversations is very different from reading books or listening to lectures.

It was agreed that I would reach out to Professor Kim. Around Lunar New Year of the new millennium, I gave him a call. I explained our history and conveyed Professor Ahn's thoughts. I said that while it might be hard to meet frequently, the three of us could still gather from time to time. I was hopeful.

After listening quietly for a while, Professor Kim finally replied, 'That all sounds wonderful… but we're all past eighty now. Who knows when one of us might suddenly pass away, following the natural order of things? Suppose one of us does pass. How would we bear the loss and grief? Wouldn't it be better to remain apart and simply read about it in the news when someone passes? That way, at least, the shock and sense of loss might be less severe. Why form deep new bonds again, only to face the inevitable?'

His voice over the phone was soft and calm.

'I suppose you're right,' I said. I asked him to call if he changed his mind.

Thinking back to the sorrow and silence that followed Professor Han's passing, I wondered whether it really was wise to take on the possibility of a great loss again. When I relayed this to Professor Ahn a few days later, he, too, replied, 'You're right. I hadn't thought of it that way.' He seemed to be reflecting on Professor Kim's advice – that in old age, it might not be wise to form deep attachments with people our age. We shared the same unspoken understanding that to go gently and quietly was perhaps the wisest path.

Half a year has passed since that conversation. I haven't heard from Professor Kim, and although I've seen Professor Ahn two or three times, neither of us has brought it up again. Perhaps the words to the old Korean song, 'Life is fleeting, don't give your heart away,' have begun to haunt us.

Just recently, I shared these thoughts with my eldest daughter. I told her I couldn't decide one way or the other.

'Whatever you do, don't be the first to go, Dad,' she advised. 'Just imagine how guilty you'd feel for the loss they'll feel.'

She smiled, but there were tears in her eyes. I could see she was thinking not of some abstract old man, but of her father. Feeling I had upset her for no good reason, I went upstairs to my room. The radio I had left on was playing the Mendelssohn violin concerto – a tune I had loved in my student days. Back then, too, I'd whispered to myself, 'All beautiful things remind me of solitude and transience.'

The Secret to My Health

I was born with a frail constitution. My family didn't believe I would ever live a normal, healthy life. My mother used to say in my presence, 'I would be happy if you make it to twenty.'

But I fought the illnesses and won. From the age of fourteen, I began to hope I might not die young after all. By the time I finished middle and high school, I was confident that with effort, I could live and work in good health. Compared to others my age now, I'm arguably doing better than most.

I'm deeply grateful that I've never been hospitalised, nor have I ever undergone surgery. I've rarely had to put my work on hold due to illness. For this, I'm beyond grateful.

At thirty, I grew confident in my ability to work in good health. After fifty, I felt I could maintain my health as well as anyone else. And by seventy, I was considered healthier than my peers.

There's no special secret to it. I simply took care of myself as though it were my duty. I needed to stay healthy in order to fulfil the tasks given to me. This resolve stemmed from a promise I made to myself in childhood. Even now, I don't seek a healthy life for its own sake, but so I can continue working.

Avoiding alcohol and cigarettes, knowing they could only be harmful, greatly contributed to my health in old age. Those born with physical vulnerabilities often have one hidden advantage: they learn early not to overexert themselves. Although I've accomplished a great deal, I always took on responsibilities slightly below my maximum capacity. If I could manage 100, I only committed to 90. That way, I'd often end up doing 120. Commit to 120, and you'll likely fall short of 100.

These days, we're bombarded with health advice from all sources. Chief among them is exercise. Unfortunately, I wasn't able to enjoy exercise until I turned fifty as I was simply too busy. I never even considered fishing, golf or hiking, all of which my friends enjoyed, because I couldn't spare the time.

After fifty, I began playing soccer with university friends. It's a rather rough sport, but I'd spent my youth in Pyongyang playing soccer, so I enjoyed it for several years. Eventually, I hit my physical limits and switched to tennis at my children's suggestion. But tennis requires coordinating schedules with a tennis partner. So, just before retirement, I began looking for a solo activity I could do anytime.

A THEORY OF HAPPINESS

Swimming was perfect. It engages the whole body and can be done at any time if there's a pool nearby. But I never overexerted myself. If I could swim 100 metres, I'd stop at 90, so that I'd want to come back again the next day. It's been over thirty years since I started swimming regularly, and I still swim almost every day. I even request hotels with pools when I travel abroad.

My biggest challenge with swimming was skin care, so I paid close attention to it. I also developed a routine that worked for me so as to avoid injuries. I swam for thirty years not because I was obsessed with maintaining my health, but simply to enjoy it, and reaped great health benefits from it. As long as there is a pool nearby, I'd like to keep swimming for a few more years.

As one grows older, walking becomes the best exercise. But rather than walking for health's sake or to exercise, I prefer to venture out to the mountain path to enjoy its beauty. Once walking becomes an everyday habit, it's so enjoyable you hardly notice you're doing it.

Still, the body inevitably ages. A friend who was a few years ahead of me once said, 'In my seventies, I aged every year. In my eighties, I could feel myself aging every month. And after ninety, I feel a little older every day.' Aging is unavoidable. But from my sixties onwards, I've found that a peaceful heart and a healthy mind improves physical stamina, too.

Though the body may age, the decline of emotional intelligence doesn't come as quickly. People often say, 'Though my body has aged, I feel just the same as before.' As we age, we must pay attention to staying young of mind and maintaining mental wellbeing. The old saying goes, 'Sound body, sound mind,' but in old age, it's perhaps more accurate to say that a strong mind sustains physical health.

Reflecting on this, I believe I've been a successful man in terms of health.

*We should strive to view life positively,
living with hope and optimism.
Persistent negative thinking leads to despair.
But a positive mindset cultivates hope.*

Health is Built Over Time

Lose your health, and you lose everything. Because health is tied to life itself.

Doctors bear the primary responsibility for this precious gift, and we are grateful for their noble service. But the secondary responsibility lies with each of us.

Most people acknowledge that after forty, mental wellbeing contributes to physical health. Since Freud, we've come to have a better understanding of psychological illnesses and that true healing is a synthesis of physical and mental care. No one denies this anymore. Excessive concern only creates more stress, but indifference isn't the answer, either. While we should take advice from doctors and other health experts, we must take charge of our own health.

Let me offer one or two suggestions based on my own journey from a sickly child to one of the healthiest among my peers as I embrace my centenarian years.

First and foremost, this means avoiding harmful habits or behaviours.

Tobacco and drugs are among the worst offenders. Narcotics are so dangerous that the law steps in. If people knew the full extent of their effects, they would recognise them as true evils. I was once shocked to learn that a clergyman I respected was a drug addict. I also witnessed the only son of a well-known public figure struggle with addiction. The responsibility to shield our youth from such harm cannot be emphasised enough.

Smoking is difficult to quit. I wouldn't presume to condemn others' vices while I am unable to give up my daily cup or two of coffee. Some say a little alcohol is fine, but cigarettes are best avoided altogether. Even doctors who once smoked usually quit by forty, because they know the risks.

I've lost more than one friend to lung cancer while they were still in their prime. I've also seen smokers lose their hearing much earlier than others. One usually does not notice the adverse effects of harmful substances until it's too late. I've lived my entire life without alcohol or cigarettes, and I'm now thankful for that. Knowingly harming your health is, in a way, a disregard for life itself.

Another unhealthy habit is overworking one's body or mind. One of my students, who was preparing to study abroad in Germany not long after getting married, went to the beach with friends. He drank with them, then impulsively jumped into the cold water and died of a heart attack. His family was devastated. I couldn't help thinking at the funeral that if he'd been born with a weak constitution like mine, perhaps such a tragedy wouldn't have happened. He would never have taken such a risk.

We take unnecessary risks often because we overestimate our strengths. Those who work within their limits tend to stay healthier, work longer and accomplish more.

One friend had severe tuberculosis in middle school. Without financial support, he might not have survived. He never played sports; short walks were all he could manage. But through careful moderation, he produced many scholarly achievements and remains relatively healthy in his late seventies. He once said that since being discharged from the hospital in middle school, he's never been hospitalised again.

It's often difficult for athletes to maintain their health into old age. Physical overexertion takes its toll. And when physical training overshadows mental discipline, that imbalance can yield negative consequences.

In the long run, the best approach is to maintain balance between body and mind. The notion that a sound body keeps the mind sound still holds true, but from forty onwards, the opposite becomes just as accurate: those with strong mental resolve are better equipped to maintain good physical health. Up until forty, it may not be difficult to maintain physical health. But as you age, emotional and psychological stress can have enormous, sometimes fatal, physical consequences.

When business fails, when a beloved family member passes, when we suffer severe social or personal shock, we cannot get through it without mental resilience. We find ourselves being dangerously serious when we say, 'I'd rather die.'

What we need in such moments is emotional stamina. And this becomes even more vital in midlife and beyond. With a strong mind, we can escape the grip of despair. Religious faith works for some; an unwavering sense of purpose helps, too. But cultivating that emotional strength takes time, and it is prudent to start working on it from a young age in order to reap the benefits in middle-age and beyond. Worldview, it goes without saying, plays an important role in this process. As the ancients said, 'Empty-handed we come, empty-handed we go.' This teaches us to let go of excessive desires and ego. Those who empty themselves as they age stay healthy not just in spirit, but in body. Once you reach sixty, you begin to understand that strong mental fortitude is what truly sustains your physical health.

Another path to health is to work. A person who loves their work is more likely to stay healthy. Work is important in midlife, and doubly so in old age.

Work enriches our lives. Those who keep moving forward through their work maintain both mental and physical health. People who work are generally healthier than those who don't, but overwork must be avoided, as it robs us of the capacity to continue our work.

Animals do not overdrink, overeat or overindulge. Even predators, when full, won't hunt prey standing right before them. They also do not mate recklessly. But humans, driven by mental desires, constantly overreach. We work for money, overextend ourselves for the sake of honour or take on positions in old age that we are no longer suited for.

Such overreaching isn't a healthy pursuit of work, but an act of personal greed. One might call it ambition, but when it exceeds one's limits, it becomes harmful to health. A person with the capacity for 100 units of work should aim for 90, doing their best. That way, they may accomplish 100 or even more. But if they attempt 120, they might not even manage 90 and will harm their health in the process.

Doing work appropriate to one's abilities greatly benefits health in old age. Seniors who remain engaged in work tend to live longer and healthier lives than those who do nothing.

There are two kinds of work: mental and physical. The more balanced they are, the better. Farmers and fishermen ought to fill the mental gap left by physical labour with intellectual pursuits, promoting both health and personal growth. For those in mental labour, it is ideal to devote some time to physical activities.

Office workers try to make up for the lack of physical activity at work with exercise. With the rise of gyms and health clubs, people often think that more exercise leads to better health. The same goes for fishing, golf and hiking. But for 100 units of health, only 90 units of exercise are needed. Excessive exercise or obsession with health can backfire. We must aim for balance.

As for me, I've always lived a busy life, so I enjoy swimming, which is a solitary activity I can do anytime. I began after sixty and have continued for over thirty years. But I never push myself. I enjoy it in a way that isn't strenuous. I don't know how much longer I'll keep swimming, but when that time comes, I'll likely switch to walking. I believe walking is the best form of exercise. Jogging when young, walking a lot after sixty and walking slowly and moderately in old age is what I consider most beneficial.

In Germany, cycling and swimming are recommended nationally. As one ages, the lower body weakens, so leg exercises become essential. I avoid using machines for exercise because they feel unnatural. That might suit young people training to be athletes, but for those in midlife and beyond, gentle, natural movement is best. After sixty, it's wise to intentionally balance work and health.

I've heard from experts that health and diet are inseparable. Two essential principles are to avoid unbalanced meals and overeating. It is widely known that unbalanced meals lead to nutritional deficiencies, and eating too much is more harmful than eating moderately.

Some advocate for strict vegetarianism or warn against certain foods, but I believe that in practice, the matter of healthy eating resolves itself naturally. It likely depends on one's constitution, but as we age, we gravitate towards plant-based foods, and often find that the body craves the food it needs.

Too much attention to food can actually be harmful. I don't believe much in tonics made in the practice of Eastern medicine, and I try to avoid taking medication in general unless absolutely necessary. Tonics might help when recovering from an illness or be useful in small amounts in old age, but taking tonics for stamina does not sit well with me. Just as excessive cosmetics can age a woman's skin over time, unnecessary tonics may weaken the body as we grow older. Most of the healthy people I know avoid tonics altogether. They don't seem to feel the need for them. In old Korea, it was often royalty who consumed the most tonics, and perhaps it's no coincidence their average lifespan was relatively short.

A good doctor prescribes medication only when necessary and avoids invasive procedures when possible. The body's natural resilience is key. Medication should support that resilience, and we should only engage with bigger interventions when they are truly necessary.

When my mother was ninety-seven, she had hip surgery. Everyone feared the surgery would put too great a strain on her. But she recovered faster than many younger patients. Perhaps it was because she had never taken medication before, so the antibiotics were highly effective. It's best to avoid medicine unless absolutely needed.

People have varying opinions about sexual activity and health. Some say less is better for one's wellbeing; others believe appropriate sexual activity supports overall health. Both perspectives have merit. But recently, many agree that appropriate sexual activity benefits health and enhances social abilities.

However, promiscuity or the pursuit of excessive pleasure degrades both character and human dignity. People who fall into such patterns often appear morally degraded, and their health tends to suffer.

As with alcoholism, being consumed by lust or compulsion is harmful for one's health and social life. Moderation, as they say, is key.

★ ★ ★

A THEORY OF HAPPINESS

Cultivate hope and optimism. Among those walking the same path in life, some only notice the darkness and obstacles, while others see light and possibility. Those with passive thoughts succumb to negativity; those with an active will and optimistic worldview stay mentally and physically healthier. Persistent negativity leads to despair, while a positive attitude creates hope.

In short, a cheerful heart and a strong will make for a healthy human being. And that wholeness supports physical health, too. Of course, none of this happens without effort, and those who are naturally positive and strong in mind are truly blessed. People of faith are often mentally resilient. That's because they believe that a higher power is watching over them.

When I was in my early forties, I went to the United States. Everything felt foreign – the towering dormitory buildings, the daily use of elevators, the unfamiliar language and customs, the noise of traffic, the feeling of isolation. I couldn't sleep well, and my digestion suffered.

I went to consult a doctor. He was a renowned physician at the University of Chicago. He asked many questions, then asked what change I would want if I were to move to Harvard. I said, first and foremost, I'd prefer to live in a one-storey house.

He diagnosed my condition as a mild form of neurosis caused by the stress of a sudden environmental change. I agreed. Later, I heard of a professor who suffered from debilitating depression due to difficulties with his research and had to be brought home by his wife. Another professor at Harvard even took his own life.

In midlife and beyond, the greatest threat becomes chronic lifestyle diseases. And the stress that creeps in during this stage of life poses a serious threat to our health. Alarmingly, signs of these lifestyle illnesses are appearing in adolescents these days.

The most frequently mentioned chronic conditions are diabetes, high blood pressure and obesity. These require individuals to act as their own physicians. Especially with obesity, careful management starting in one's late thirties can produce lasting results.

People use different methods. Among the people I've met, some have run consistently for twenty years, while others have consumed specific health foods for over a decade. These efforts suggest that lifestyle diseases require long-term solutions spanning fifteen to twenty years. And if one can regain one's health, isn't that worth it?

The Hunza region is often cited as home to a population with the longest life expectancy in the world. It's said they share three key traits: lifelong physical labour from an early age, a diet free from chemical additives and an innately optimistic personality. Notably, lifestyle diseases are extremely rare there. Illness, in the end, may be something we bring upon ourselves.

Some people ask how much rest and sleep are needed for good health. I believe in rest for the sake of work, not rest for rest's sake. If we rotate between different types of tasks rather than stick with one activity for too long, we do not need to take long breaks. Sleep is described as the rest of all rests. Anyone who has experienced insomnia will understand what a blessing a good night's sleep truly is.

From my experience, short rest breaks and moderate sleep are best, especially when it becomes a routine. You don't have to live a rigidly scheduled life, but living itself is for the sake of work. And appropriate rest to support that work is itself a blessing and the path to health. In this light, perhaps the best health is the fruit of self-discipline and character. Health isn't so much a gift as something we build.

*Life is not a road that leads to death,
but a path to completion.
Death does not rob us of everything,
but gives our lives an ending that completes the
story of our lives.
And the complete story is the legacy we leave
after we are gone.*

Another Name for Death: Life

In Buddhism, human life is understood as a cycle of birth, aging, illness and death.

No one knows what lives we lived before we were born, nor do we know what the afterlife looks like, because we did not exist before birth, and we will cease to exist when we die. All that belongs to us is the time we are given between birth and death. What comes before or after is not for us to know.

Yet if we examine more closely, even the life after birth doesn't immediately belong to us. For a while, we have biological existence with little awareness of it. Life only truly becomes ours when we have both physical and mental lives. This is why individuals suffering from severe mental illness or dementia may be considered to not be living fully – their cognitive function is impaired.

Human beings are not born with any intention or purpose of their own. Some philosophers describe human existence as something randomly thrown into the world. But once this 'thrown being' gains self-awareness, life becomes a series of choices rather than coincidences. One's life is shaped by one's own will from this point onwards. The being cast into the world becomes the centre of gravity in his life. The being journeys through life, forging deep attachment to living and creating meaning of absolute value.

The process of life – growing up and growing old, falling ill, dying – might seem uniform and predetermined if viewed purely in physical terms. But if we look at the mental and spiritual dimensions, life is not the same for everyone, nor does it unfold according to a fixed plot. Each person lives out a different, original narrative.

Still, no matter what that story may be, it all ends with death. That cannot be avoided. Death ends every part of life. What once was becomes no more. Our lives end for us when we die.

Yet death does not come to us as an *inevitability* but an *absolute certainty*. Death, in fact, is not an incident that *seeks us out* but a direction that life is headed. One might say we live to one day die. But that is the approach of a person who writes down the answer without showing the work. For such a person, death may not be the *purpose* of life, but perhaps the *end*.

Most of us prefer not to think about death. Embedded deep within the essence of existence is the wish to not die and live forever. Regardless, we continue down the path to death. That is life. Life and

A THEORY OF HAPPINESS

death do not coexist; they are mutually exclusive by nature.

And yet, death dwells within life. Because it has no other place to dwell. That is why we humans live with unease, fear and despair as part of our daily existence. Death, nesting within life, cultivates anxiety and hopelessness. It threatens our very being.

Still, that approaching shadow never disappears. In life's most shining moments, death whispers in our ears. As young newlyweds on their honeymoon dream about their future, death soundlessly asks, *Can you say for certain that you'll get to see this place again?*

For most of us, our earliest encounters with death are indirect. We read about someone dying in the newspaper. Then, someone we know dies, and the reality of death draws closer. Eventually, a loved one passes, and it feels as if a piece of one's own life has vanished. When someone you loved as deeply as yourself dies, it's as if the root of your life and the foundation of your being has ripped out from under you. Death is experienced much more directly then.

Finally, death creeps up on us. And when that happens, anxiety turns to fear, and we descend into the pit of despair as we confront the futility of our efforts. Yet even then, we do not *experience* death itself because we are not granted the chance to experience death and come back to reflect on it. We may experience the pain that leads to it, or the process of approaching its door – but death itself remains unknowable. We die, but we do not know death.

Still, let us attempt to distinguish between two aspects of death: the body and the mind. Physically, death arrives at the end of biological function. As death marks the cessation of life, it is crossing the threshold into nothingness.

Our consciousness also dies with the body, but the fruits of the mind's labour live on. Socrates was sentenced to death, but his belief in justice did not die with him. If anything, his death empowered that belief to move future generations. Jesus died on a cross, but his spirit continues to guide the course of human history. Great or small, many lives have left behind hope and light because of the meaning found in their death.

From this perspective, our physical lives *stop* with death, but our legacies are given an ending and become *complete* with death. When Jesus said from the cross, 'It is finished,' it was a confession that his death fulfilled and completed his life's purpose.

I once knew an artist who was battling cancer. He knew well that his cancer was going to claim his life, but decided that he would be the one to write the ending. He tied his unresponsive upper body to a chair and continued to paint the picture he had wanted to complete. He died after laying down his brush. What he sought was to not give up, to spend his final days well, with dignity and purpose. Death brings closure to the story and meaning of our lives. If completion is fulfilment, then a life without death cannot be complete.

Life does not move towards death, but towards completion. Death does not merely take everything from us, but allows us to leave behind the fruits of our life's work. It is through death that we leave something behind, just as parents leave an inheritance to their children. Through death, we bequeath our legacy to society. In this way, we survive among our fellow humans. Our lives, after coming to an end in time, continue in history.

But how long should a person live?

Our physical instincts might answer: the longer, the better. Perhaps we wish death didn't exist. But what would the consequences be? It's said that the Japanese have the longest average lifespan. But there are reportedly over a million registered cases of dementia in Japan, and perhaps five times as many unregistered ones. A life that becomes a burden to others is not ideal.

When Somerset Maugham turned 90, he confessed to reporters that he'd gotten sick of his tiresome and dreary life. Spending old age with limitations, fatigue and suffering cannot be pleasant. The wiser among the elderly accept their physical end as peacefully as the sun setting in the western sky.

So, if we ask our spiritual, intelligent selves how long we ought to live, we might say, 'For as long as we can enjoy life and be of help to others.' If living is no longer joyful or meaningful, then the will to live fades. The most basic condition for joy and happiness in life is the ability to serve a purpose. It may not matter as much in our youth, but in old age, the greatest loss is the loss of work. A life without work is neither good for oneself nor for others. A life that causes pain or burden to others brings no fulfilment. It only causes suffering for those who love us. Of course, we cannot control life and death at will. But if we can live long enough to work and help others, that would be a life to be thankful for. A valuable life in old age is still possible if we find joy in work and meaning in helping our loved ones. So perhaps we should not desire merely to live long, but to live with purpose in old age.

One of the most respected figures of the twentieth century was Dr Albert Schweitzer. He was a world-renowned musician and a pastor. He was so brilliant that he could have become a professor by his mid-twenties. But he gave it all up to become a physician, dedicating his life to caring for the sick in Lambaréné, present-day Gabon. His writings and service to the world was inspired by his reverence for life.

In a letter to a friend, shortly before his death at over ninety years old, he wrote: 'No one is more blessed than I am, as I was able to serve suffering patients for over sixty years. If you hear news of my passing, please don't grieve, but celebrate my life.' Schweitzer tended to his patients in Gabon to the very end. Young doctors urged him to rest, but he asked them not to rob him of his happiness.

Trajectory and work of his life were important, but more valuable were the example and lessons he left behind – a life that inspires humanity to build a good and meaningful society for generations to come. A life that *others* hope will continue is a precious life. But a life *I* greedily wish to extend is not a life lived in wisdom.

They say a tiger leaves behind its pelt when it dies, but a human leaves behind their name. For animals, it is enough to leave behind something useful. But for humans, what matters is the legacy of spirit. By 'name', we do not mean just a label or personal identifier. It stands as a symbol of our accomplishments and spiritual heritage. Had Admiral Yi Sun-sin left no legacy, his name would be meaningless. His legacy, and the value of it, are measured by what he left behind after death. That is the spiritual inheritance we received from his death.

Naturally, we need not bother evaluating lives that were meaningless or morally bankrupt. There are 'necessary evils' in the world that function as cautionary tales, and some argue that evil can exist as part of a process. But what we seek is the good and the opportunity to create more good in the world.

Throughout the long history of humankind, we have inherited many legacies, most of them material. Wealth, businesses and properties passed down by pioneers in commerce and industry continue to provide the foundation for our lives, contributing to our economic wellbeing. Politicians and engineers who have left behind legacies of governance or innovation fall into this category as well.

In contrast, there are those whose gifts were spiritual. The intellectual and moral leaders such as scholars, thinkers and artists left behind non-material legacies.

Those who dealt in material things could enjoy their wealth during their lifetimes. But those who gave us spiritual inheritance often did so for the sake of others. Those who have little and give much, unlike those who have much and give little, receive our deepest respect and thanks.

There are also those who left no fortune and no business empire, who were neither scholars nor artists, but who lived lives devoted to service. Good physicians devote themselves to the health of the community. Good educators pour their soul into nurturing upright citizens. Such lives spent caring for others earn the gratitude and respect of many.

If we consider the people who most exemplified this spirit of service, we may include sages like Confucius, the Buddha and Jesus. Confucius was not a scientist like Einstein. The Buddha did not possess Beethoven's musical genius. Jesus left behind no writings like Plato's. And yet, we revere them more deeply than any scientist or artist, and we do not compare them with successful tycoons or political leaders. The reason is simple: they were teachers who taught human beings how to live.

The world mourned the death of Mother Teresa. There are hospitals in Africa today that are much larger than the one Dr Schweitzer built. But Schweitzer and Mother Teresa are honoured not because they received the Nobel Peace Prize, but because they practised and shared the most noble form of love. They were the highest expression of compassion. Their minds carried the spirit of sacrifice for the sake of love. Material inheritance brings material wealth; cultural legacy brings cultural abundance. But love is what truly guides our lives.

We are born to live our best lives so that we may leave behind something valuable, and we die so that our gifts may be passed on.

Does this mean that cultural and spiritual legacies are more worthy than material ones? No. Rather than judge a person by their occupation or social role, we should assess how much they helped others through their lives. Some people in business serve others generously with their wealth. And there are religious leaders who bring harm and sorrow in the name of their gods. In modern society, we continue to see religious conflicts and doctrines that lead to widespread harm – hardly an example of service or contribution to humanity. The most foolish and unfortunate life is one lived solely for personal pleasure or wealth, especially when that selfishness causes others pain. In contrast, a life lived in service to others, for the sake of their wellbeing and dignity, leaves behind a noble legacy. That is why people have long asked not only how someone lived, but also how they died. One may die a disgraceful, empty death, or a noble and honourable one. Death is the summary of a person's life and the final criteria by which we evaluate that life.

Still, we cannot say death itself is the destination of life. But we can say that, in contrast to death that comes passively or inevitably, there is such a thing as a meaningful, noble death – one that is chosen. The great people who shaped history were often those who chose such a death. To them, death may have represented the highest aim of life itself. History refers to such deaths as martyrdom. Martyrs chose death in pursuit of a higher, more noble life.

Many figures in world history gave their lives freely for their countries. Admiral Yi Sun-sin lived for his country and died for it, thus fulfilling his great purpose. Gandhi lived for the people of India and died for them. His death gave his life even greater meaning, and his spiritual legacy continues to shine in India and beyond.

The Night Train of Life

Here's a story I once heard: We are all passengers on a night train, travelling the long journey of life. It is an endless journey stretching across tens of thousands of years. Each passenger on this train must eventually disembark. Some ride for fifty years, some for sixty or seventy, others for a full hundred, but when the train arrives at their station, each must get off. Outside the train, it is pitch dark. No one, not even the traveller himself, knows where they are going once they step off.

To get off the train of life means to step out into death. And no one knows what lies beyond it. Most people try hard to avoid getting off at their station. They plead, 'How can I leave my family?' They ask, 'Where am I supposed to go in such utter darkness?' But when the time comes, everyone must leave the night train. The train moves on without pause, indifferent to who has disembarked or what has become of them. Two people may choose to get off at the same time, but each must go off on their own separate path the moment they step off the train. Coexistence is allowed only on the train, within the boundaries of life. We are all riding this night train of life. In a hundred years, everyone on board now will have been replaced. Even in fifty years, half the faces we know will have stepped off into the darkness.

There was a man named A on this train. While on board, he worked tirelessly to earn money. With that money, he bought valuable possessions, ate good food and dressed in fine clothes. Time passed. He grew old and the time came for him to step off the train. But he didn't want to. How could he leave behind the money he had scrimped and saved, so frugally that he couldn't find a single bowl of rice to spare for a hungry stranger? How could he hand over all the treasures he had clutched so tightly, never letting go for a single moment? As he agonised, the train pulled into his station. It was time. A hugged his possessions one last time before being pulled off the train out into the darkness, where there was nothing but night. His family stayed behind and divided up his money, his belongings, his food. They said, 'He was a generous father.' But the passengers still on the train looked on in silence. One of them said quietly, 'He loved his wealth so dearly. I can't imagine how much it hurt that he couldn't take it with him.'

There was another man on the train, named B. He had spent his life devoted to art. In his youth, he endured poverty and frequently went hungry. He never lived in luxury. He had only a few friends, with whom he shared warm companionship. But still, he managed to publish a few volumes of his works. He had little interest in money or material goods. In winter, he got by in a threadbare coat. In summer, sweat poured from his brow as he wrote. Eventually, his time came too. He said goodbye to his few friends, quietly remarking, 'I wish I had left behind better work…' And then he stepped off the train. As the train moved on, the remaining passengers read his books. They said, 'He lived a hard life, but gave us so much joy. We're thankful to him.'

There was also a man called C. He spent nearly his whole life walking up and down the train. He sought out the sick to offer comfort and medicine. He visited those who were suffering and lent them a sympathetic ear. Sometimes he gave his own food to someone poorer than himself. Sometimes, without a word, he sat beside someone just to sit with them in their sorrow. His whole life was love and service. To everyone, he offered the same smile, the same kindness, the same compassion. It was as if he had boarded the train to serve the abandoned and forgotten. When his time came, he too stepped off the train. Many mourned his departure. 'If only he could have stayed with us a little longer.' One passenger said, 'We should carry on his work and help those in need as he did.'

Which of these three people would we like to be? How should we live our lives?

How Long Should a Person Live?

A few years ago, a young professor I knew passed away at the age of forty-nine. It was a heartbreaking loss for all.

One of our colleagues said, 'He should've lived at least until sixty. It was far too soon.' Because he died in the prime of his working life, the grief felt heavier.

But if everyone lived for as long as they wished, wouldn't that cause its own problems? Wouldn't it lead to more and more versions of 'Goryeojang' – the Goryeo dynasty custom of leaving the elderly in the woods to die? The world would be overrun with the old.

Of course, a long, healthy life is what everybody wants. But if life becomes a long illness, then death may be the natural release from suffering. Then, considering health and other conditions, how long should a person live?

At the very least, people want to live for as long as the national average. There is nothing wrong with wanting to live as long as others do. But try telling someone who has already outlived the average, 'You've lived long enough – you can die now.' Even those in their nineties don't want to die. Long life remains one of humanity's greatest and deepest desires.

Whenever I ponder this, I recall something a friend and Eastern-medicine doctor once said: 'If I reach a point where I can no longer work, no longer help anyone, and my strength is gone, then it would be better for me to welcome death.'

He passed away a few years after he became a widower. He was still young enough to work.

Another memory comes to mind: I once overheard a mother visiting her son in prison. Her son had killed a friend at the age of nineteen. The mother was consumed by despair. She murmured, 'If only I had never given birth to that child…' If a parent can spend her life ashamed of her beloved child, perhaps a long life isn't always a blessing.

Having witnessed these things, I've come to realise that the meaning of life is bound to the question of death. What does my life mean to others? If we reach a point where our work is done and we can no longer be of help to others, perhaps we should receive death with gratitude.

Then perhaps the desire to live long should be replaced with the desire to do as much work for the world as we can. Rather than staying healthy for one's own sake, we should use our health to offer even the smallest kindness to others. The true question is not about the physical vessel that contains us, but what we fill that vessel with. If our health allows us to work and help others, then a long life is a blessing, and one to be celebrated.

Life and death are not ours to control. If everything went according to our plans, what would we have to worry about? No one looks their loved ones in the eye and calmly says, 'It's time for me to go.' No one simply decides, 'I've lived enough. I will die now.' Death always comes from outside us. It is not our decision.

Still, one cannot deny that striving until the very end, to live in a way that brings joy and assistance to others is a most beautiful and worthy goal.

A Note on the Author

Professor Kim Hyung Seok is a 105-year-old first-generation Korean philosopher. A former Harvard research professor, he has found true happiness in life, having overcome adversity from a young age, and is committed to spreading joy and helping others through his work. He was born in and grew up in the North Korean province of South Pyongan before leaving to study philosophy at Choson University in Japan. To this day, he remains engaged with lecturing, broadcast and writing.